CITY WILDLIFE GUIDE

REPTILES OF SYDNEY

SNAKES, LIZARDS AND TURTLES OF THE GREATER SYDNEY REGION

CHRIS WILLIAMS
AND TIM FAULKNER

Published in 2026 by Reed New Holland Publishers

newhollandpublishers.com

A record of this book is held at the National Library of Australia.

ISBN 9781760796983

Managing Director: Fiona Schultz
General Manager: Olga Dementiev
Publisher and Project Editor: Simon Papps
Designer: Andrew Davies
Production Director: Arlene Gippert

Keep up with Reed New Holland and New Holland Publishers
NewHollandPublishers
@newhollandpublishers and @ReedNewHolland

Front cover: Red-bellied Black Snake (PETER SOLTYS).

Back cover (clockwise from top left): Macquarie Turtle (MARK SANDERS), Common Bandy Bandy (MARK SANDERS), Eastern Water Dragon (MARK SANDERS), Broad-tailed Gecko (LUCAS WILLIAMS).

Page 1: Blotched Blue-tongue (PETER SOLTYS).

Pages 2–3: Eastern Water Dragon (PETER SOLTYS).

CONTENTS

INTRODUCTION

Reptiles of the Greater Sydney region

Sydney is often hailed as one of the world's most vibrant and liveable cities, but beyond the skyline and surf lies a complex and dynamic natural landscape teeming with native wildlife, including more than 70 species of reptiles. Stretching from the Pacific Ocean in the east to the Blue Mountains in the west, and encompassing escarpments, heathlands, wetlands and remnants of urban bushland, the Greater Sydney region supports a surprisingly rich and varied diversity of reptile life. This biological wealth is not just confined to remote bushland but reaches deep into the suburbs, often unnoticed by many residents.

Whether it's an Eastern Water Dragon basking beside a stormwater canal, a Red-bellied Black Snake slipping through creek-side vegetation, or a host of small skinks, many of which have adapted to life in backyards perhaps more successfully than in their original bush habitats, reptiles are woven into the very fabric of suburban and natural environments alike. Some species, such as the familiar Eastern Blue-tongue, have adapted remarkably well to the pressures of urban expansion and habitat modification. Others, for example the elusive and endangered Broad-headed Snake, remain highly specialised and vulnerable, clinging to survival in the sun-warmed sandstone outcrops of areas of isolated bushland.

This book is your guide to meeting these animals where they live. It's designed for local people, tourists, bushwalkers, students, educators and anyone curious about the scaly neighbours that inhabit Sydney's parks, bushland, waterways and gardens. The pages offer insight into the fascinating reptile species that call Sydney home – and how best to observe and appreciate them.

Understanding the region

The Greater Sydney region spans a broad ecological range, shaped by its humid subtropical climate and varied terrain. From sea cliffs and mangroves to upland ridges and dry woodland, each habitat supports a distinct community of reptile species.

Seasonal activity

Reptile behaviour is closely tied to temperature and season:

- **Summer (Dec–Feb):** Warm and humid, peak time for reptile activity, including basking, breeding and feeding.

- **Autumn** (Mar–May): Activity slows with cooling temperatures, but sightings remain common on warm days.
- **Winter (Jun–Aug)**: Many species brumate, but some, such as blue-tongues and Red-bellied Black Snakes, may still be seen basking on sunny days.
- **Spring** (Sep–Nov): Activity surges with rising temperatures. Mating, nesting and hatchling emergence begin.

Zones and distribution

To simplify how we present species distributions across this diverse region, we've divided Greater Sydney into **five ecological zones**. These are referenced in each species profile and illustrated on the inside front cover:

- **Zone 1 – Sydney Basin**
- **Zone 2 – Illawarra**
- **Zone 3 – Southern Highlands**
- **Zone 4 – Blue Mountains**
- **Zone 5 – Central Coast**

Rather than using detailed range maps, we have indicated the zones where species are *most often encountered*. This offers a practical, reader-friendly approach suited to the regional scope of the guide.

Zone summaries

Zone 1: Sydney Basin and Cumberland Plain

Covering key centres including Sydney, Parramatta, Blacktown, Penrith, Campbelltown and Liverpool, the Cumberland Plain lies at the heart of the Sydney Basin and supports some of the highest reptile diversity in the region. Once dominated by open grassy woodland and grassland, the area has been heavily modified by urban development. Nevertheless, remnant bushland, parklands and suburban green space continue to support a range of reptile species.

Species such as Eastern Water Dragon, Eastern Blue-tongue, Golden-crowned Snake and Red-bellied Black Snake remain common and are often encountered in gardens and reserves, and even along railway corridors. These adaptable reptiles highlight the resilience of native fauna within a fragmented and highly urbanised landscape.

Zone 2: The Illawarra

The Illawarra – stretching from Helensburgh to Kiama and including towns such as Wollongong, Shellharbour, Thirroul, and Dapto – is characterised by cool temperate forests, coastal escarpments, and broad sandy beaches. Its mix of sandstone formations and sheltered gullies supports a diverse reptile fauna. The Broad-headed Snake, an endangered species, occurs in sandstone outcrops and sheltered woodlands, although it is now rare and of significant conservation concern in the region. Other notable species include the Heath Monitor, which is found in heathlands and open forest, and the Gully Shadeskink, which inhabits moist, shaded gullies, particularly in the northern Illawarra.

Zone 3: The Southern Highlands

Encompassing towns such as Bowral, Mittagong, Moss Vale, Robertson and Bundanoon, the Southern Highlands are defined by rolling plateaus, temperate woodlands and deep gorges. With a cooler climate and consistent rainfall, the region supports reptiles that favour moist and shaded conditions. The White-lipped Snake is well suited to the heath and open woodland areas. The Southern Water Skink is another key species – it is often seen along streams and among rock piles. The region's forested valleys and escarpments are vital strongholds for these species and other reptiles often overlooked in broader conservation narratives.

Zone 4: The Blue Mountains

Encompassing towns such as Katoomba, Leura, Blackheath, Springwood and Lithgow, the Blue Mountains are defined by steep cliffs, deep valleys and sandstone ridges. These features create a mosaic of cooler microclimates that support a diverse reptile fauna.

The Blue Mountains Water Skink, an endangered species endemic to the area, inhabits swampy headwaters and sedge-rich valleys. The Mountain Dragon is commonly seen basking on rocky slopes and in open woodlands. Another notable species is the Eastern Three-lined Skink, which thrives in open forests and heathlands, often sheltering under rocks and logs.

Zone 5: The Central Coast

Extending from the Hawkesbury River and Mooney Mooney Bridge in the south through to Lake Munmorah in the north, the Central Coast encompasses towns such as Woy Woy, Somersby, Gosford, Terrigal, Avoca Beach and The Entrance. This region marks the southernmost reach of subtropical rainforest in Australia. Shaped by a warm, humid climate, the area supports rich biodiversity across its dunes, estuaries and coastal forests. The Copper-tailed Skink is commonly seen darting through sandy heath and open forest. The Eastern Water Skink thrives along creek lines and garden edges, while the Robust Velvet Gecko emerges at night to forage on tree trunks, rocks and even house walls. The area's wetlands, mangroves and forest margins offer important refuges for a wide array of both terrestrial and semi-aquatic reptiles.

Key habitats of the Sydney region

1. Urban parks and gardens

Pockets of vegetation in suburban areas – including remnant bushland, landscaped gardens and golf courses – can support generalist and adaptable species. These habitats often host Eastern Blue-tongue, Eastern Water Dragon and small skinks such as those in the genus *Lampropholis*.

2. Grassland

Open grassy areas are often found on urban fringes, roadside verges, or in modified paddocks, occasionally with scattered trees or shrubs. These areas support species such as Three-toed Skink and Eastern Morethia.

Zones: Zone 1 – Sydney Basin
Zone 3 – Southern Highlands
Zone 4 – Blue Mountains

3. Sandstone escarpment and mountains

Dramatic cliff lines, plateaus and rugged terrain found predominantly in the Blue Mountains and Ku-ring-gai area. These complex rock formations and dry heathlands support specialists such as Broad-headed Snake, Jacky Dragon and velvet geckos.

Zones: Zone 1 – Sydney Basin
Zone 2 – Illawarra
Zone 4 – Blue Mountains

4. Wetlands and estuaries

Freshwater and brackish environments such as lagoons, reedbeds, mangroves and creek margins. Reptile life includes Eastern Long-necked Turtle, Red-bellied Black Snake and Water Skink.

Zones: Zone 1 – Sydney Basin
Zone 2 – Illawarra
Zone 5 – Central Coast

5. Subalpine heath and swamp

Cooler, elevated areas above 600 metres, typically in the Southern Highlands and higher elevations of the Blue Mountains. These areas are characterised by dense low shrubs, sedgelands and seasonal swampy patches. Species here include the Mountain Dragon.

Zones: Zone 3 – Southern Highlands
Zone 4 – Blue Mountains

Habitat List

Habitat type — **Representative regions**

HERBERT HEINSCHE/SHUTTERSTOCK.COM

1. Urban parks and gardens — Sydney region

TIM FAULKNER

2. Open grasslands and swamps — Southern Highlands, Cumberland Plain

TIM FAULKNER

3. Sandstone escarpments Illawarra, Blue Mountains, Central Coast

TIM FAULKNER

4. Wetlands and estuaries Central Coast, Illawarra, Sydney

TIM FAULKNER

5. Subalpine heath and swamp Blue Mountains (higher elevations)

Using this book

How species entries are structured

Each species account includes the following information:

Common and scientific species names

Reptile taxonomy is dynamic, with names changing as new data – particularly genetic – becomes available. To ensure consistency, we've followed the **Official List of Australian Species** (28 May 2025), maintained by the Australian Society of Herpetologists (ASH):
www.australiansocietyofherpetologists.org/official-list-of-australian-species

Where multiple common names exist, we've chosen those most widely recognised in NSW.

Venom rating

To keep things simple, snakes are grouped into three categories based on the potential risk their venom poses to humans:

Highly venomous – Species capable of delivering a bite that, without prompt medical treatment, carries a high risk of death.

Venomous – These snakes inject venom when they bite. It has been proven that the effects of the exact same bite on different people can vary greatly, so anyone bitten by a venomous snake should always seek immediate medical attention.

Non-venomous – Species that do not possess venom. They do, however, have teeth and can still deliver a painful bite.

Marsh Snake

LUCAS WILLIAMS

Species status – how it's determined

Conservation listings in this guide draw from:

- The **IUCN Red List**, which reflects global status
- Some species may be listed as 'Least Concern' globally but are rare or declining locally. Where such differences exist, we provide context in the Notes section to clarify the species' true conservation outlook in the Sydney region.

Urban Occurrence Ratings explained

☆☆☆☆☆: 0 stars – Rarely encountered in urban settings

★☆☆☆☆: 1 star – A species that is still entirely reliant on its natural habitat, although that habitat is now in proximity to urban environments.

★★☆☆☆: 2 stars – A species that will venture into urban environments but will not typically live long or stay there if given a chance to leave.

★★★☆☆: 3 stars – A species that may be surviving in an urban environment, although its numbers are declining.

★★★★☆: 4 stars – A species that has demonstrated the ability to adapt and thrive in urban environments as effectively as it does in the wild.

★★★★★: 5 stars – A species that has shown it may be more successful in an urban environment than in the wild (a synanthropic species).

- **WHEN AND WHERE** – Likely time and conditions for sightings.
- **DESCRIPTION** – Size measured as snout-vent length (SVL) and total length (TL) in mm; also carapace length (CL) in mm for turtles. Key field features are described, such as body shape, colour and markings.
- **DISTRIBUTION ZONES** – Listed by number (1–5), showing areas of common occurrence.
- **HABITAT** – Summary of environments where the species is typically found.
- **NOTES** – Behaviour, ecological interactions and identification challenges.
- **REPRODUCTION** – Egg-laying (oviparous) or live-bearing (viviparous), and clutch data if known.

Ethical herping

Exploring the wild to observe reptiles – known as 'herping' – can be an exciting and educational experience, but it must be done responsibly.

Key ethical guidelines include:

- Observe, don't disturb. Avoid handling unless absolutely necessary.
- If lifting habitat items (for example, rocks), return them *exactly* as found.
- Never remove animals, rocks or vegetation.
- Respect the land – this is ancient country with deep cultural and ecological significance.

Some reptiles, such as the Broad-headed Snake, rely on specific rock habitats that can be destroyed by careless behaviour. Ethical herping ensures these fragile ecosystems remain intact for future generations.

Community and connection

Sydney is home to a vibrant herpetological community. Established in 1949, the Australian Herpetological Society (AHS) is the oldest of its kind in the country and welcomes members of all experience levels. Monthly meetings feature guest speakers whose presentations cover a wide range of topics, appealing to both beginners and seasoned enthusiasts.

The society holds a scientific licence and organises regular field trips during the warmer months – ranging from short morning or afternoon excursions to extended expeditions lasting up to a week in remote locations.

Membership benefits include free or discounted entry to some of Australia's top wildlife parks and zoos, as well as a subscription to the *Red Bellied Courier*, the AHS's full-colour journal of more than 100 pages.

The AHS hosts monthly meetings, talks and field activities:

- Woodstock Community Centre, 22 Church St, Burwood, NSW 2134.
- Fourth Wednesday of each month, 7.30pm start.
- Website: www.ahs.org.au
- Email: info@ahs.org.au

Whether you're an expert or a newcomer, getting involved is a great way to learn, contribute to conservation and connect with others who share your interest in reptiles.

Broad-tailed Gecko

MARK SANDERS

MARK SANDERS

Blotched Blue-tongue

Acknowledgements

The authors extend their sincere gratitude to the many people who contributed to the making of this book. In particular, we thank Rob Ambrose, Mitchell Hodgson, Sandra Trujillo, Mark Sanders, Jules Farquhar and Rick Shine for their valuable advice on species selection, image choices and the inclusion of key information throughout the project.

A heartfelt thank you goes to all the photographers who generously shared their images, whether or not they appear in these pages. We believe that wildlife photographers are the unsung heroes of herpetology, and their work deserves far greater recognition than we can give here.

Tim would like to acknowledge the staff at the Australian Reptile Park, whose enthusiasm and commitment continue to inspire him every day. Chris extends his thanks to the dedicated network of catchers across Urban Reptile Removal and Sydney Snake Catcher, whose professionalism and passion for both reptile welfare and public education are a constant source of motivation. These men and women are on the ground every day, helping people to understand and appreciate the privilege of sharing their backyards with reptiles.

Our sincere thanks also go to Simon Papps, Fiona Schultz and the entire team at New Holland Publishers for their continued and unwavering support of our projects.

We also acknowledge the members of the Australian Herpetological Society, whose shared enthusiasm for reptiles continues to strengthen this community. For more information on meetings and field trips, visit www.ahs.org.au.

And finally, to our families – thank you for your patience, encouragement and unwavering support of our many reptile-related projects. This book simply wouldn't exist without you.

NEXT SPREAD: Eastern Blue-tongue in Balmain East. (ANDY MONCK)

SPECIES ACCOUNTS

Eastern Long-necked Turtle *Chelodina longicollis*

JULES FARQUHAR

STATUS: IUCN Least Concern; Urban Occurrence Rating ★★★★★

WHEN AND WHERE: Common in slow-moving waterways and dams throughout Greater Sydney. Frequently seen crossing roads during rain events in summer.

DESCRIPTION: CL 254mm. Medium-sized turtle with elongated neck and slightly flattened head. Plastron (underside of the shell) noticeably expanded at front, extending past inner edges of marginal scutes of carapace. Upper shell rich brown to dark brown or black, while underside varies from white to cream or brown with bold black seams. Juveniles often display striking black and orange-red markings on plastron.

DISTRIBUTION ZONES: 1, 2, 3, 4 and 5.

HABITAT: Lakes, swamps, slow-moving rivers and farm dams.

NOTES: Undergoes significant overland migrations, often resulting in vehicle casualties. Citizen-science initiatives are actively relocating turtles from roads to nearby water bodies. Emits a pungent musk when threatened.

REPRODUCTION: Female lays up to three clutches per season, each containing up to 25 brittle-shelled eggs. Nesting occurs from late spring to early winter.

Macquarie Turtle *Emydura macquarii*

MARK SANDERS

STATUS: IUCN Least Concern; Urban Occurrence Rating ★★★☆☆

WHEN AND WHERE: Most active during warmer months. Often observed basking on rocks or logs in early morning sun.

DESCRIPTION: CL 189–340mm. Freshwater turtle with short neck and small head. The shell, which is serrated in juveniles, is broadly oval and flares at rear. Upper shell fawn to light brown; underside cream to pale yellow. A pale stripe runs from lower jaw along each side of neck. Each forelimb has five claws.

DISTRIBUTION ZONE: 1.

HABITAT: Primarily found in large, slow-moving river systems in eastern Australia. Also occurs in major lakes and artificial water bodies.

NOTES: Local Sydney subspecies *dharuk* is is found in Nepean River. Genetic studies reveal distinct catchment populations, although subspecies-level resolution remains difficult. The release of pet turtles into the wild poses a serious threat to local genetic integrity through hybridisation.

REPRODUCTION: Mates in spring. Female lays up to three clutches of 30 eggs between September and January, usually after heavy rain on warm, overcast evenings. Hatchlings emerge around February.

Red-eared Slider *Trachemys scripta elegans*

GARY STEPHENSON

STATUS: **Introduced non-native species**; IUCN Least Concern (globally); NSW declared pest species; Urban Occurrence Rating ★★★★★

WHEN AND WHERE: Bask on logs or rocks near water bodies in spring and summer.

DESCRIPTION: CL 300mm. Medium-sized freshwater turtle with dark green to brown shell, often featuring yellowish markings. A distinctive red stripe runs behind each eye.

DISTRIBUTION ZONES: 1, 2 and 5.

HABITAT: Prefers freshwater lakes, ponds and slow-moving rivers.

NOTES: Native to USA but introduced worldwide. In NSW has been recorded in urban waterways. Populations are established in some areas, especially in slow-moving or still water bodies. This highly invasive species competes with native turtles, such as the Eastern Long-necked Turtle, for resources and nesting sites. It is often released by pet owners, contributing to its spread. Known for aggressive basking behaviour, pushing native turtles off logs. NSW authorities strongly discourage ownership due to its environmental impact.

REPRODUCTION: Females lay multiple clutches of 10–30 eggs per year, typically in spring or summer, which hatch after 60–90 days, depending on temperature.

Lesueur's Velvet Gecko *Amalosia lesueurii*

SHANE BLACK

STATUS: IUCN Least Concern; Urban Occurrence Rating ★★☆☆☆

WHEN AND WHERE: Shelters beneath rocks or in crevices by day. Most active at night, particularly in summer, emerging to hunt insects and small arthropods.

DESCRIPTION: SVL 80mm, TL 130mm. Medium-sized gecko with flattened body, long tail, and wide digits tipped with adhesive pads and small claws. Dorsal colouration varies from pale grey to brown with a **subtle zigzag pattern along spine.** Skin has a fine, velvety texture due to microscopic scales.

DISTRIBUTION ZONES: 1, 2 and 4.

HABITAT: A rock-dwelling species that inhabits caves, exfoliating rock surfaces, and crevices in sandstone formations. While typically associated with rocky habitats, it can also be found in dry sclerophyll forests.

NOTES: A key prey species for the endangered Broad-headed Snake. Uses its flattened body to squeeze into narrow rock crevices for shelter and protection from predators. Often confused with Eastern Stone Gecko.

REPRODUCTION: Females lay two eggs in communal nesting sites, often within rock crevices. Multiple clutches may be produced in a single breeding season.

Eastern Stone Gecko *Diplodactylus vittatus*

MARK SANDERS

STATUS: IUCN Least Concern; Urban Occurrence Rating ★★★★★

WHEN AND WHERE: Nocturnal, most commonly observed in spring and summer, especially after rain.

DESCRIPTION: SVL 62mm, TL 85mm. Small, robust gecko with smooth velvet-looking appearance Back is brown or grey, marked with **high contrasting pale zig-zag or series of blotches along the spine. Pattern often extends onto head, forming light cap**. Flanks usually have pale, unbordered spots.

DISTRIBUTION ZONES: 1, 3 and 4.

HABITAT: Dry woodlands, grasslands, shrublands and forests. Commonly shelters under rocks, logs or leaf litter, or in soil cracks or burrows.

NOTES: When disturbed, emits distinctive squeaking sound as a defence. Like many Australian geckos, can also drop tail if threatened, which later regenerates.

REPRODUCTION: Two leathery eggs laid in summer, typically in December or January. Communal nesting sites occasionally observed.

Robust Velvet Gecko *Amalosia robusta*

MARK SANDERS

STATUS: IUCN Least Concern; Urban Occurrence Rating ★★★★★

WHEN AND WHERE: Nocturnal, typically seen in warm months, especially after rain.

DESCRIPTION: SVL 80 mm, TL 170 mm. Grey to dark brown body with pale blotches along back and distinctive tail used for fat storage. **Regenerated tail mottled and lacks original pattern.** Skin soft and velvety, typical of velvet geckos. Flattened body helps it to fit under bark or within rock crevices.

DISTRIBUTION ZONES: 5.

HABITAT: Dry sclerophyll forests and woodlands; often shelters in rock outcrops, caves and loose bark. Can enter buildings, especially near bushland edges.

NOTES: More robust than many geckos. Often remains motionless when disturbed. May be confused with other velvet geckos, but thick tail and bold behaviour help with identification. Like other geckos, it can shed its tail as a defence strategy. The regrown tail is smooth and lacks original markings.

REPRODUCTION: Lays two eggs at a time, with multiple clutches produced each season, often in communal nesting.

Broad-tailed Gecko *Phyllurus platurus*

LUCAS WILLIAMS

STATUS: IUCN Least Concern; Urban Occurrence Rating ★★★★☆

WHEN AND WHERE: Primarily nocturnal, most active in the warmer months, often found on rock faces and brick walls.

DESCRIPTION: SVL 95mm, TL 165mm. **Flattened body with broad tail and cryptic patterning.** Grey with darker mottling spots or flakes. No distinctive pale bands on tail, though original tail may have irregular bands towards extreme tip. **Broad, leaf-shaped tail resembles head** and acts as decoy against predators.

DISTRIBUTION ZONES: 1, 2, 3, 4 and 5.

HABITAT: Sandstone outcrops, rocky escarpments, and occasionally in urban environments, where well adapted and inhabit brick walls and rock gardens.

NOTES: A master of camouflage, often flattening against rock surfaces to become almost invisible. When threatened, may shed tail as a defensive mechanism.

REPRODUCTION: Mating occurs in May, with females laying one or more clutches between November and January. Eggs are typically laid in deep rock crevices or cavities in brick walls. Communal nesting is known. Females will use the same nest site each year if possible. Hatching occurs from January to April.

Thick-tailed Gecko *Underwoodisaurus milii*

MARK SANDERS

STATUS: IUCN Least Concern; Urban Occurrence Rating ★★★★★

WHEN AND WHERE: Nocturnal, active in warm months, often after rain.

DESCRIPTION: SVL 100 mm, TL 156 mm. Varies in colour from brownish to purplish-brown, covered in large cream or yellow spots that often align along spine to form loose bands. **Head typically has pale markings, especially on snout, lower jaw and neck base.** Original tail is thick, black and ringed with 5–6 bold white bands. Regrown tail is smooth, blunt and mottled in colour.

DISTRIBUTION ZONES: 1, 2 and 3.

HABITAT: Rocky outcrops, dry forests and shrublands. Commonly shelters under bark, rocks or logs, and occasionally uses burrows. Individuals sometimes form small groups in shared daytime retreats, potentially aiding in thermoregulation.

NOTES: When threatened, emits a loud bark-like call and raises tail in arched defensive posture. Unusually cold-tolerant for a gecko, it can persist in cooler regions of southern Australia.

REPRODUCTION: Two hard-shelled eggs per clutch, often in communal nest sites, hatching after about 65 days. Can lay several clutches between July and February.

Asian House Gecko *Hemidactylus frenatus*

SHANE BLACK

STATUS: **Introduced non-native species**; IUCN Least Concern; Urban Occurrence Rating ★★★★★

WHEN AND WHERE: Nocturnal. Active year-round in warm climates, but sightings increase in summer months. Commonly seen on walls near lights at night.

DESCRIPTION: SVL 55mm, TL 115mm. Slender, agile gecko with granular skin and small spines along tail. Varies from pale pinkish-grey to light brown, often mottled; belly white. Long toes with distinct pads for climbing vertical surfaces.

DISTRIBUTION ZONES: 1 and 5.

HABITAT: Widespread in urban and suburban environments further north of Sydney. In tropical regions can number in the hundreds on a single building; also found in woodlands and disturbed areas. Frequently shelters in crevices of buildings, under bark, or inside sheds and letterboxes.

NOTES: Native to South-East Asia, now naturalised in Australia, particularly in warmer regions. Makes distinctive chirping calls at night, which are often mistaken for those of crickets. Highly adaptable and can outcompete native geckos.

REPRODUCTION: Lays two small, hard-shelled eggs at a time, in a secure, hidden locations. Breeding can occur multiple times a year in warmer regions.

Burton's Legless Lizard *Lialis burtonis*

SHANE BLACK

STATUS: IUCN Least Concern; Urban Occurrence Rating ★★★★★

WHEN AND WHERE: This nocturnal species is commonly observed during the warmer months crossing roads in suitable habitats.

DESCRIPTION: SVL 290mm, TL 800mm. **Easily recognisable by long, pointed, wedge-shaped snout** and fragmented head shields. Pupils are vertical and oval-shaped, and has very small limb flaps. Appearance highly variable, with many different colours (grey, brown, yellow or red) and patterns found in same area.

DISTRIBUTION ZONES: 4 and 5.

HABITAT: As the most widely distributed member of its family, it occurs throughout most Australian habitats. Present in all environments within Greater Sydney region. A terrestrial species whose primary food source is small skinks.

NOTES: A specialised predator, feeding almost exclusively on other lizards, particularly skinks. Uses flexible skull joints to swallow relatively large prey whole. Prolific in parts of northern Australia. Sightings within Greater Sydney normally the result of chance encounters rather than by successfully targeting the species.

REPRODUCTION: Two eggs are laid at a time, with multiple clutches being laid over the warmer months.

Common Scaly-foot *Pygopus lepidopodus*

MARK SANDERS

STATUS: IUCN Least Concern; Urban Occurrence Rating ★★★★★

WHEN AND WHERE: Nocturnal; active in warmer months. Often seen crossing roads.

DESCRIPTION: SVL 274mm, TL 840mm. Wide variation in colour, but in Sydney region usually grey or red-brown with grey head and tail. Tend to have faint markings, with a few displaying blotches, although some traces of blotching are often still visible on tail. Distinct black line under eye. Scales strongly keeled.

DISTRIBUTION ZONES: 1, 4 and 5.

HABITAT: Dry woodlands, grasslands, heaths and areas with long grass. Commonly found in leaf litter, under rocks and within long grass, seeking shelter during day and becoming active at dusk.

NOTES: May be confused with Eastern Brown Snake due to similar appearance. When threatened, may display defensive behaviours such as flicking tongue and mimicking snake-like movements to deter predators. Can be distinguished from snakes by presence of external ear openings, a broad, fleshy tongue, and a long tail that comprises a significant portion of its body length.

REPRODUCTION: Two eggs laid at a time. Multiple clutches can be laid in a single season, and communal nest sites are known.

Red-throated Skink *Acritoscincus platynotus*

MARK SANDERS

STATUS: IUCN Least Concern; Urban Occurrence Rating ★★★★★

WHEN AND WHERE: Most active in warmer months, particularly spring and summer, when emerges to forage and bask. Common in Hills District but rarely seen.

DESCRIPTION: SVL 80mm, TL 200mm. Small, slender skink with silver-grey or brown dorsal surface and bold dark lateral stripe running from snout to tail. **Throat normally tinged orange**, with colour more intense in male. Juvenile often has bright red throat; colour fades with age but remains visible in both sexes.

DISTRIBUTION ZONES: 2 and 4.

HABITAT: Diurnal, sun-loving species that prefers areas with abundant leaf litter, logs and rock slabs for shelter. Often found on rocky sandstone ridges, where it hides in crevices or under stones. When disturbed, it will dart rapidly into cover.

NOTES: Sexual dimorphism is evident, with males exhibiting a brighter red throat, particularly in breeding season. Sometimes confused with the Eastern Three-lined Skink, but the red throat in both sexes helps distinguish it.

REPRODUCTION: Up to 12 eggs laid in communal nesting sites beneath logs and rocks in December or January. Eggs hatch within 6–8 weeks; juveniles disperse quickly to avoid predation.

Eastern Three-lined Skink *Acritoscincus duperreyi*

JULES FARQUHAR

STATUS: IUCN Least Concern; Urban Occurrence Rating ★★★★★

WHEN AND WHERE: Diurnal, seen basking on logs, rocks and exposed ground in spring and summer. Actively forages during the day.

DESCRIPTION: SVL 80mm, TL 200mm. Silver-grey to greyish-brown, usually with prominent pattern. **Narrow dark stripe runs along spine, bordered by thin, pale stripes with dark inner edges.** Broad black stripe above white mid-lateral stripe run along side. Throat orange-red, variable in intensity, being most vivid in males during breeding season. Juveniles may appear more vividly marked.

DISTRIBUTION ZONE: 3.

HABITAT: Common in open woodlands, grasslands, alpine meadows and suburban gardens. Shelters under logs, rocks, leaf litter and debris such as tin sheets.

NOTES: Egg incubation temperature influences sex determination. Higher temperatures result in mostly female offspring, while lower ones produce more males. This species is a well-known example of temperature-dependent sex determination and is used in climate change research due to its sensitivity.

REPRODUCTION: Up to 10 eggs laid in moist, sheltered microhabitats, sometimes in communal nests, in early to mid-summer, hatching from late summer.

Punctate Worm Skink *Anomalopus swansoni*

MARK SANDERS

STATUS: IUCN Data Deficient; Urban Occurrence Rating ★★★★★
WHEN AND WHERE: Year-round, although rarely seen due to fossorial habits. Most records unearthed during excavation or under debris following rain.
DESCRIPTION: SVL 107mm, TL 200mm. Limbless, elongated skink with a smooth, glossy body and a blunt snout tipped with a waxy scale. Eyes very small and external ear openings absent, reflecting its adaptation to life underground. Dorsal colouration varies from pale to dark brown, often uniform or very faintly patterned. Ventral surface lighter – often cream or pale pinkish.
DISTRIBUTION ZONE: 5.
HABITAT: Loose, sandy or loamy soils in dry sclerophyll forests, open woodlands, coastal heaths and native grasslands. Typically found beneath logs, bark or stones, or within deep leaf litter. May shelter in termite mound or invertebrate burrow.
NOTES: Can be confused with small species of blind snakes (*Anilios* spp.), juvenile legless lizards, or worm-like skinks such as *Lerista*.
REPRODUCTION: Live young. While specific data on its litter size is limited, a related species, *Anomalopus pluto*, has an average litter size of 2.5 offspring. This suggests that *A. swansoni* may have a similar reproductive pattern.

Land Mullet *Bellatorias major*

MARK SANDERS

STATUS: IUCN Least Concern; Urban Occurrence Rating ★★★★★

WHEN AND WHERE: Spring to autumn. Most active during warmer months, especially morning and late afternoon. Often seen basking on walking tracks or foraging in leaf litter after rain.

DESCRIPTION: SVL 300mm, TL 700mm. Back and sides uniform dark brown to black, and **adult has distinct pale ring around eye**. Juvenile has bold cream or bluish-white spots along sides. Underside varies from white to orange-brown.

DISTRIBUTION ZONE: 5.

HABITAT: Rainforests, wet sclerophyll forests and dense coastal or montane undergrowth, usually near watercourses or in gullies with thick leaf litter. Tolerates disturbed areas such as forest edges and gardens if adequate cover is available.

NOTES: Juveniles have been observed staying with their mother for up to 12 months before eventually dispersing and becoming independent.

REPRODUCTION: Gives birth to 5–9 live young in late summer or early autumn. Young are precocial and often remain close to mother for extended periods, exhibiting limited parental association, which is uncommon among skinks.

Elegant Snake-eyed Skink *Cryptoblepharus pulcher*

JULES FARQUHAR

STATUS: IUCN: Least Concern; Urban Occurrence Rating ★★★★★
WHEN AND WHERE: Most active in warmer summer months. Often seen in suburban gardens and parks, and on buildings. Basking behaviour makes it easily observed.
DESCRIPTION: SVL 41mm, TL 100mm. Flattened body and long limbs. Eyes hav fixed, clear scale (spectacle) instead of movable eyelids. Upper body copper-brown to silver-grey, with a narrow cream to yellow stripe running along each side from above eye to tip of tail; stripe is bordered by black. Top of head coppery brown.
DISTRIBUTION ZONE: 1.
HABITAT: Naturally adapted to rocky outcrops and tree trunks. Has colonised urban structures, such as brick walls, fences, sheds, and retaining walls; now more commonly seen on suburban brick walls than in its original natural habitats.
NOTES: Highly adaptable and often the dominant skink species in urban areas. Actively forages on vertical surfaces for ants, spiders and other small invertebrates. Quick to flee but often returns to the same basking site when undisturbed.
REPRODUCTION: Lays around three eggs during spring and summer. Eggs typically deposited deep within rock crevices or, more commonly, in cracks within brick walls. Communal nesting is common.

Copper-tailed Skink *Ctenotus taeniolatus*

JULES FARQUHAR MARK SANDERS

STATUS: IUCN Least Concern; Urban Occurrence Rating ★★★★★

WHEN AND WHERE: Most active during warmer months. Frequently encountered on ranges, escarpments and rocky scree.

DESCRIPTION: SVL 80mm, TL 200mm. A long-tailed skink with **a coppery-orange tail and a black stripe running along its side to the tip.** The body is rich brown with dark and pale stripes running from the snout down the back and sides. The limbs are reddish with black streaks, and the underside is pale whitish. Juvenile lacks reddish colours.

DISTRIBUTION ZONES: 4 and 5.

HABITAT: Found in a variety of environments, including coastal heath, dry woodland and sclerophyll forest, generally associated with rocky terrain.

NOTES: Has not adapted well to urban environments. More commonly found on urban fringes and in bushland than in suburbia. Often confused with Eastern Striped Skink and White's Skink.

REPRODUCTION: Mating occurs in spring and early summer, with females laying clutches of up to seven eggs.

Eastern Striped Skink *Ctenotus robustus*

MARCUS HEALEY

STATUS: IUCN Least Concern; Urban Occurrence Rating ★★★★★

WHEN AND WHERE: Active spring to early autumn, especially on warm, sunny days.

DESCRIPTION: SVL 123mm, TL 250mm. **Prominent stripes and large scales inside leading edge of ear opening.** Back pale to dark brown or olive-brown, with broad black stripe edged in white or cream running from neck to tail. Pale stripe extends from above eye to tail, bordered by black stripe above and dark brown band below with pale spots. Limbs well developed, streaked or striped with dark brown, and underside whitish.

DISTRIBUTION ZONES: 1 and 4.

HABITAT: Occupies diverse environments, including sandy heaths, rocky outcrops and grasslands. Utilises rocks, logs and ground litter for shelter, and creates burrows under rocks for hibernation and nesting.

NOTES: Highly active and fast. Often seeks refuge under logs or in deep leaf litter when disturbed. May be confused with Copper-tailed Skink, which has a similar appearance but differs in specific markings.

REPRODUCTION: Up to nine eggs laid in early summer, hatching in late summer.

Pink-tongued Skink *Cyclodomorphus gerrardii*

JULES FARQUHAR

STATUS: IUCN Least Concern; Urban Occurrence Rating ★★★★★

WHEN AND WHERE: Most active in warmer months, particularly spring and summer.

DESCRIPTION: SVL 200mm, TL 450mm. Large head distinct from neck, long prehensile tail and pink tongue in most adults. Body colour ranges from pale brown, pinkish-brown, to grey, with a variable pattern.

DISTRIBUTION ZONES: 4 and 5.

HABITAT: Moist environments such as wet sclerophyll forests, rainforest edges and suburban gardens; often near water sources and in leaf litter. Semi-arboreal, frequently climbing low vegetation, using long, semi-prehensile tail for support.

NOTES: Nocturnal. When threatened, displays pink tongue in defensive posture similar to its blue-tongues. Often mistaken for Eastern Blue-tongue, but can be distinguished by its elongated body, pink tongue and dark snout tip.

REPRODUCTION: Live bearer. Give birth to litters of 20–25 young in early summer, which are born curled up in a fetal membrane that they consume after birth. Juveniles have a blue tongue, which changes to pink in about three months.

Mainland She-oak Skink *Cyclodomorphus michaeli*

BRIAN LA RANCE

STATUS: IUCN Not Evaluated; Urban Occurrence Rating ★★★☆☆

WHEN AND WHERE: Most active in **spring and summer**, particularly after rain. **Diurnal** but tends to stay hidden under cover, so sightings relatively uncommon.

DESCRIPTION: SVL 126mm, TL 350mm. Fairly large, elongate skink with smooth scales and strong tail. Varies from reddish-brown to olive or grey, often with paler flanks and underbelly. Juvenile may have more distinct dark lateral stripes or flecks. Dark stripe often runs from snout, through eye, and fades along side of neck. Snout tip often darker than the rest of head. Limbs short but well developed.

DISTRIBUTION ZONES: 4 and 5.

HABITAT: Rocky hillsides, grassy open forests and sclerophyll woodlands, especially with dense ground cover, leaf litter or fallen timber. Prefers well-drained soils and patchy vegetation. Can persist in modified landscapes with suitable cover.

NOTES: Secretive. Often found sheltering beneath fallen timber or in crevices.

REPRODUCTION: Viviparous. Mates in early spring; female gives birth to 8–15 young in mid- to late summer, which are fully formed and independent at birth.

Cunningham's Skink *Egernia cunninghami*

MARK SANDERS

STATUS: IUCN Least Concern; Urban Occurrence Rating ★★★★★

WHEN AND WHERE: Cold-tolerant. Avoids heat. Can be found all year round, especially basking in the cooler spring and autumn seasons. Often found in high-traffic tourist locations/lookouts.

DESCRIPTION: SVL 200mm, TL 450mm. Large, robust skink with thick, spiny tail. Each scale on back and sides each has a short, sharp spine, becoming longer and more prominent on tail. Upper body grey-brown to olive-brown, often with paler flecks. In Sydney region, tends to be paler, with hints of pink and cream on belly.

DISTRIBUTION ZONES: 3 and 4.

HABITAT: Rock escarpments, ranges and ridges throughout entire Greater Sydney region. Always associated with rock and most commonly found near exfoliating rock shelves. Prefer habitats with ample crevices and shelter.

NOTES: Relatively common within its preferred habitat and range, typically found on granite outcrops. Colonies exhibit a notably advanced social structure for lizards. In captivity, has been known to live for more than 40 years.

REPRODUCTION: Up to 10 live young are born in summer.

Tree Skink *Egernia striolata*

JULES FARQUHAR

STATUS: IUCN Least Concern; Urban Occurrence Rating ★★★★★

WHEN AND WHERE: Active year-round, especially when sunny. Most often seen in spring and summer. Diurnal. Basks on rocks or logs in morning or late afternoon.

DESCRIPTION: SVL 119mm, TL 250mm. Stout body, flattened head and tail, keeled blunt scales, and strong limbs with five toes. Back pale grey or dark grey or brown, often with small pale spots. Neck and shoulders paler; **dark stripe runs from eye to hips.** Head scales usually have dark edges. Some individuals have broken lines along back from neck to tail. Underside pale orange, dull yellow, or silver-grey, with dark bars on chin and throat and dark speckles on chest.

DISTRIBUTION ZONE: 4.

HABITAT: Rocky outcrops, tree hollows and ground debris in open forests.

NOTES: Frequently seen basking on vertical tree trunks, rocky ledges or logs. Highly site-faithful, often using same crevice or hollow for extended periods. Diet mainly invertebrates, along with some plant material such as leaves and flowers.

REPRODUCTION: Viviparous. Mates in spring, with around five live young born in late summer. Juveniles often remain with the parents for extended periods, contributing to their social group structure.

Yellow-bellied Water Skink *Eulamprus heatwolei*

PETER SOLTYS

STATUS: IUCN Least Concern; Urban Occurrence Rating ★★★☆☆

WHEN AND WHERE: Active in warmer months, particularly in spring and summer. Often seen basking on rocks, logs or other sunlit surfaces near water bodies.

DESCRIPTION: SVL 100mm, TL 200mm. Sleek, robust skink with streamlined body. Dorsal colour ranges from olive-brown to dark brown, often with darker speckling along back and sides. Flanks dark with lighter spots, and belly bright yellow, extending up to throat, which is white with black marbling.

DISTRIBUTION ZONES: 2 and 4.

HABITAT: Found near streams, creeks and rocky outcrops in sclerophyll forests, woodlands and montane regions. Prefers sunny areas close to water.

NOTES: Distinguished from other *Eulamprus* skinks by its white throat with black marbling and a bright yellow belly – these are key traits that separate it from *E. quoyii*, which lacks throat patterning. Also differentiated by a pale stripe that begins behind the eye but ends at the mid-back, unlike the longer, continuous stripe of the Eastern Water Skink.

REPRODUCTION: Mating occurs in spring, with females typically giving birth to litters of up to eight offspring in late summer.

Eastern Water Skink *Eulamprus quoyii*

ROB AMBROSE

STATUS: IUCN Least Concern; Urban Occurrence Rating ★★★★★

WHEN AND WHERE: Most active in warmer months, especially from spring to early autumn. Often basks near water, particularly in morning and late afternoon.

DESCRIPTION: SVL 115mm, TL 300mm. Varies from olive-brown to dark brown, with black speckling and pale stripes along body. Flanks darker, sometimes with blotches. Belly cream to yellow, sometimes with a golden hue in breeding season.

DISTRIBUTION ZONES: 1, 2, 3, 4 and 5.

HABITAT: Streams, rocky creeks, rainforest margins, wet sclerophyll forest and riverbanks. Highly adaptable to disturbed and urban environments; common in parks, gardens, drains and artificial ponds – often seen in city bushland reserves.

NOTES: One of the most commonly seen skinks in eastern Australia. Highly alert and fast moving; will often dive into water or retreat under cover when approached. Pale yellow dorsolateral stripes extend well beyond shoulder, helping to separate it from *E. heatwolei* and *E. tympanum*. Lacks throat marbling and has longer tail and larger body than other water skinks in region. Diet includes insects, worms, spiders and occasionally plant matter or carrion.

REPRODUCTION: Mates in spring; litter of to up to nine offspring born in summer.

Blue Mountains Water Skink *Eulamprus leuraensis*

MARK SANDERS

STATUS: IUCN Endangered; Urban Occurrence Rating ★★★★★

WHEN AND WHERE: Spring to early autumn. Endemic to Blue Mountains region; very localised distribution, confined to discrete montane peat-swamps in this area.

DESCRIPTION: SVL 70mm, TL 200mm. Dark brown to black dorsal colouration, featuring **narrow yellowish-bronze or white stripes running along back and continuing onto tail as a series of spots**. Head bronze to brown with black markings; flanks and limbs dark with yellowish spots. Underparts cream with small dark markings. The overall darker colouration and distinctive striping make it unlikely to be confused with other *Eulamprus* species in the region.

DISTRIBUTION ZONE: 4.

HABITAT: Montane wetlands, dense vegetation near creeks, and swampy heathlands.

NOTES: A habitat specialist confined to high-altitude montane swamps in the Blue Mountains, this species is one of the few Australian reptiles entirely dependent on wetland environments. Highly susceptible to threats such as urban expansion, altered hydrology, invasive species and increased fire frequency.

REPRODUCTION: Approximately six live young are born in late December.

Southern Water Skink *Eulamprus tympanum*

MARK SANDERS

STATUS: IUCN Least Concern; Urban Occurrence Rating ★★★☆☆

WHEN AND WHERE: Active from spring to early autumn, particularly on warm, sunny days. Diurnal. Often seen basking near water bodies.

DESCRIPTION: SVL 85mm, TL 200mm. Dorsal colour ranges from olive-brown to dark brown, often adorned with dark spots or blotches. Sides are similarly coloured but feature paler speckles. A distinctive characteristic is a **pale marking that curves around the front and upper edge of the ear opening.** Unlike some related skink species, lacks continuous stripes running along back and sides.

DISTRIBUTION ZONE: 4.

HABITAT: Woodlands, rocky creeks and riparian zones. Prefers areas with ample sun exposure near permanent water bodies, often hiding under rocks, logs or plants.

NOTES: Easily distinguished from *Eulamprus quoyii* and *E. heatwolei* by absence of continuous pale dorsolateral stripes and presence of diagnostic pale crescent-shaped marking curving around front and upper edge of ear opening (tympanum). Typically found in cooler upland areas.

REPRODUCTION: Mates in spring; litter of about five offspring born in late summer.

Eastern Earless Skink *Hemiergis talbingoensis*

JULES FARQUHAR

STATUS: IUCN Least Concern; Urban Occurrence Rating ★★★★★

WHEN AND WHERE: Active from spring to autumn, although sightings are infrequent due to its fossorial (burrowing) lifestyle.

DESCRIPTION: SVL 60mm, TL 250mm. Small, slender lizard with reduced limbs, each bearing three toes. Body colour varies from pale grey to chocolate brown, often **featuring a series of thin stripes along body**. Ventral surface notably bright yellow. **Lacks external ear openings**, an adaptation associated with burrowing.

DISTRIBUTION ZONE: 4.

HABITAT: Prefers shady and damp places, often inhabiting southern-facing slopes and gullies. Typically found beneath leaf litter or logs, or within loose, damp soil.

NOTES: Reduced limbs and elongated body facilitate efficient movement through soil and leaf litter, resulting in a snake-like locomotion. Consequently, it may be mistaken for a legless lizard or small snake, or for Three-toed Skink. Often found cohabiting with small black ants, which are considered a preferred food source. When disturbed, it will quickly burrow into the soil to evade predators.

REPRODUCTION: Ovoviviparous. Females produce eggs that develop internally, culminating in the birth of 1–6 live young, usually during the warmer months.

Gully Shadeskink *Saproscincus spectabilis*

PORTIA WILLIAMS

STATUS: IUCN Least Concern; Urban Occurrence Rating ★★★★★

WHEN AND WHERE: Seen in spring and summer, particularly after rain.

DESCRIPTION: SVL 59mm, TL 110mm. Brown above, either uniform in colour or with a mix of paler and darker scales. **A dark, irregular stripe runs along each side of back, at least near the head.** Flanks may be faintly or noticeably darker, sometimes with a pale stripe along middle. Underside varies from white to bright lemon yellow. In more boldly patterned individuals, these flecks align along the scales, forming faint, streak-like markings.

DISTRIBUTION ZONE: 1.

HABITAT: Moist forests, rainforest edges and wet sclerophyll forests, often in cool, shaded gullies. Typically found within leaf litter, under logs or among rocks – places providing essential cover from predators.

NOTES: Agile climber, often found in low vegetation or within leaf litter, making it hard to spot. May be distinguished from Weasel Skink by its pale or cream upper lip, absence of a cream eye-spot, lack of orange-red dorsolateral stripe, and generally more contrasting body markings. Feeds on small invertebrates.

REPRODUCTION: About 6–9 eggs are laid in summer.

Weasel Skink *Saproscincus mustelinus*

BEN STUBBS

STATUS: IUCN Least Concern; Urban Occurrence Rating ★★★★☆
WHEN AND WHERE: Active in spring and summer, particularly when warm and humid. Diurnal. Often forages or darts through leaf litter or ground debris.
DESCRIPTION: SVL 55mm, TL 105mm. Small and slender with long tail and well-developed limbs, each with five toes. Dorsal colour light brown to gold, often with scattered pale flecks. Distinctive **cream-white spot present at corner of eye**, and orange-red stripe runs along side of tail, originating above hind limbs and extending to tail tip. Ventral surface white with a yellow flush on abdomen.
DISTRIBUTION ZONES: 1, 2, 3, 4 and 5.
HABITAT: Moist forests, woodlands and shaded rocky outcrops. Common in leaf litter, under logs and beneath rocks. Notably, has adapted well to suburban gardens, often using vegetation, compost bins and fallen timber for shelter.
NOTES: Agile climber. Often seen moving through leaf litter when disturbed. The shade skinks are slower moving then many of the other 'garden skinks' and often display a more deliberate, creeping style of movement.
REPRODUCTION: Oviparous, laying up to four eggs. Females often use communal nest sites, under timber piles or within leaf litter, that can hold more than 50 eggs.

Iridescent Litter Skink *Lygisaurus foliorum*

MARK SANDERS

STATUS: IUCN Least Concern; Urban Occurrence Rating ★★★★★

WHEN AND WHERE: Year-round, but more active during warm months.

DESCRIPTION: SVL 39mm, TL 80mm. Small, slender skink with brown to greyish-brown body, fine white speckling along sides, and dark flecks or bars on lips. Key feature is horizontally elongated ear opening, often with one or more small lobes or flaps. Notably, lower eyelid fused, forming transparent scale (spectacle) in place of movable eyelid. **Iridescent sheen can be a helpful distinguishing characteristic.** When breeding, male may develop pink to orange flush on throat and tail.

DISTRIBUTION ZONE: 1.

HABITAT: Moist forest environments, favouring forest floors rich in leaf litter and decaying logs. Considered uncommon in Greater Sydney region, but has been recorded in specific localities such as Castlereagh Nature Reserve to west of city.

NOTES: This species' secretive nature and reliance on leaf litter make it an integral component of the forest-floor ecosystem, contributing to nutrient cycling and serving as both predator and prey within its habitat.

REPRODUCTION: On average, one to three eggs are laid during summer.

White's Skink *Liopholis whitii*

JULES FARQUHAR

STATUS: IUCN Least Concern; Urban Occurrence Rating ★★★★★

WHEN AND WHERE: Most active in warm months, particularly spring and summer.

DESCRIPTION: SVL 113mm, TL 310mm. Has both striped and plain-backed forms. Striped form features broad rusty-brown stripe down spine, with dark brown to black stripes on either side, enclosing a series of pale spots. Pale stripes run along upper sides. **Flanks usually paler and greyer, with large pale spots edged in dark and a dark vertical bar above forelimb**, often containing one to three pale spots.

DISTRIBUTION ZONES: 1, 4 and 5.

HABITAT: Open woodlands, heaths and rocky outcrops. Often found in burrows or hollow logs, or under rocks.

NOTES: Known for its social behaviour, often forming stable family groups that share burrows. These groups typically consist of one male and multiple females. They are swift moving and, when disturbed, quickly retreat to their shelters.

REPRODUCTION: Viviparous. Mating takes place in September–October; 1–4 live young born in late January–February.

Eastern Morethia *Morethia boulengeri*

MARK SANDERS

STATUS: IUCN Least Concern; Urban Occurrence Rating ★★★★★

WHEN AND WHERE: Spring and summer.

DESCRIPTION: SVL 47mm, TL 100mm. Highly variable, but generally grey or brown with dark flecks. **Thin white stripe runs from mouth to groin, bordered by thicker black stripe**. Underside mostly white, while juvenile has red-orange tint under tail. Also features square-shaped scales above the eyes.

DISTRIBUTION ZONE: 4.

HABITAT: Open woodlands, grasslands and rocky outcrops. Rarely encountered in region, but may occur in drier western fringes of Greater Blue Mountains area, particularly in grassy or shrubby woodland and dry open forests. Favours habitats with abundant ground cover such as leaf litter, fallen timber and small rocks.

NOTES: Active and fast-moving. Often basks on log or rock, darting for cover if disturbed. Primarily an inland species; common just south of Canberra.

REPRODUCTION: Breeds in spring and early summer, laying about three eggs per clutch. May lay multiple clutches in a season.

Delicate Skink *Lampropholis delicata*

JULES FARQUHAR

STATUS: IUCN Least Concern; Urban Occurrence Rating ★★★★★

WHEN AND WHERE: Common in a wide variety of habitats, including suburban gardens, throughout greater Sydney region in warmer months.

DESCRIPTION: SVL 51mm, TL 105mm. Back usually brown or greyish-brown, often with dark and light flecks and streaks. May have narrow, sometimes broken, pale stripe running along back and sides. **Sides of body typically dark brown to black, with a white stripe** that can be either very noticeable or faint, but upper and lower sides always clearly defined. Underside cream.

DISTRIBUTION ZONES: 1, 2, 3, 4 and 5.

HABITAT: Adapted well to urban life and likely more common in these places than in 'wilder' areas. Prefers leaf litter, logs and rocks Often known as 'garden skink'.

NOTES: Agile and quick-moving, darting between rocks and leaf litter. Staple prey item for many small predators. Distinguished from Garden Skink (*L. guichenoti*) by slimmer build, glossier appearance, and less sharply defined striping along back and sides. Pale stripe along flank often weak or discontinuous.

REPRODUCTION: Lays eggs from September to February. Female typically produces a single clutch per year, with up to seven eggs, averaging around three to four.

Garden Skink *Lampropholis guichenoti*

JULES FARQUHAR

STATUS: IUCN Least Concern; Urban Occurrence Rating ★★★★★

WHEN AND WHERE: Common in a wide variety of habitats, including suburban gardens, throughout Greater Sydney region in warmer months.

DESCRIPTION: SVL 48mm, TL 100mm. Brown to grey, with hints of copper on head, dark speckles and pale scales. Scale edges appear rough and ragged. Dark stripe runs along back from neck to base of tail. **Sides dark brown to black, with faint pale stripe above and bolder pale stripe running along middle of sides.**

DISTRIBUTION ZONES: 1, 2, 3, 4 and 5.

HABITAT: Like some relatives, has adapted extremely well to life in suburban areas. Often seen in parks, gardens and residential and commercial areas. Relatively abundant in these places year-round; often seen sunning itself in cooler months.

NOTES: Very fast and hard to catch. Plays crucial role in controlling urban insect populations. Uses communal basking spots. Distinguished from Delicate Skink (*L. delicata*) by sturdier frame, more muted sheen, and clearer contrast between dorsal and lateral markings. Dark stripe on spine usually runs from neck to tail.

REPRODUCTION: Mates in late winter; lays clutch of about four eggs in spring. Often uses communal nesting sites, with some containing more than 200 eggs.

Bar-sided Forest Skink *Concinnia tenuis*

TOM FRISBY

STATUS: IUCN Least Concern; Urban Occurrence Rating ★★★★☆

WHEN AND WHERE: Spring and summer

DESCRIPTION: SVL 85mm, TL 200mm. Ranges from copper-brown to pale brown, with small black blotches that vary in density. Narrow dark stripe typically present on back of neck. Along upper sides, **a broad black stripe with deep pale notches often appears as vertical bars.** Tail has numerous irregular, narrow dark bands.

DISTRIBUTION ZONES: 1 and 3.

HABITAT: Notable adaptability to urban sites. Common in gardens, parks and other green spaces in established Sydney suburbs. In natural settings, favours forest, rainforest and dense woodland. Often shelters off ground in hollow logs and rock crevices. Semi-arboreal, frequently basking in dappled sunlight. Known for its agility, quickly retreating to nearby hollows or crevices when disturbed.

NOTES: Often co-occurs with Water Skink (*Eulamprus quoyii*), although it typically stays higher in vegetation or on logs, reducing direct competition and allowing it to exploit different microhabitats within the same urban green space.

REPRODUCTION: Mates in late summer; about seven live young born soon after.

Tussock Skink *Pseudemoia pagenstecheri*

JULES FARQUHAR

STATUS: IUCN Least Concern; Urban Occurrence Rating ★★★★★

WHEN AND WHERE: Active in warmer months. Often basks on rocks or grass.

DESCRIPTION: SVL 50mm, TL 115mm. **Slender body**. Highly variable colour and pattern across range. Back brown to olive-brown, sometimes with darker spots or faint stripes. **Male has orange mid-lateral stripe that is brighter during mating season.** Belly pale cream.

DISTRIBUTION ZONE: 4.

HABITAT: Prefers grasslands, heathlands and open forests, often sheltering under rocks or logs, or in dense vegetation.

NOTES: Often overlooked due to small size and cryptic behaviour. Distinguished from other small skinks by continuous reddish-orange stripe along flank, which is bordered above by a fine dark line. Known to form small groups under shelter sites, particularly in cooler or wind-exposed areas, likely for thermoregulation.

REPRODUCTION: Mates in late summer and autumn. Female can store sperm over winter, and so fertilisation occurs in spring. Up to eight young born late summer.

Southern Grass Skink *Pseudemoia entrecasteauxii*

MARK SANDERS

STATUS: IUCN Least Concern; Urban Occurrence Rating ★★★★★

WHEN AND WHERE: Spring and summer.

DESCRIPTION: SVL 75mm, TL 175mm. Grey or brown dorsal surface has darker longitudinal flecks. **Thin white stripe runs from mouth to groin on each side, bordered above by thicker black stripe.** Ventral side is mostly white. During breeding season, male has orange hue on chest and belly.

DISTRIBUTION ZONE: 3.

HABITAT: Grasslands, heaths and woodlands, particularly in areas with moist soils and dense ground vegetation. Often found beneath rocks, logs, tussocks and leaf litter. Prefers cooler climates. Found at a range of elevations, including mountains.

NOTES: Highly social – often basks in groups. Differs from *Pseudemoia pagenstecheri* in size and ventral colour patterns. Has hybridised with *P. pagenstecheri* and *P. cryodroma* where ranges overlap; this is more frequent in disturbed habitats.

REPRODUCTION: Viviparous; 3–5 live young born late summer. Female develops complex placenta-like structures to nourish embryos during gestation – a trait that has made this species a model organism in reproductive biology research.

Three-toed Skink *Saiphos equalis*

SHANE BLACK

STATUS: IUCN Least Concern; Urban Occurrence Rating ★★★★★

WHEN AND WHERE: Rarely observed due to fossorial nature, but occasionally seen in leaf litter or compost, especially following rainfall.

DESCRIPTION: SVL 120mm, TL 210mm. Elongated smooth cylindrical body with small eyes and very short limbs, each with three small toes. Dorsal shiny copper-brown to grey, with fine black longitudinal lines and black-tipped tail. Flanks and tail blackish-brown. Ventral surface yellow to yellow-orange.

DISTRIBUTION ZONES: 1, 2 and 5.

HABITAT: Moist leaf litter, soil and rotting logs in forests and woodlands. Often found in suburban gardens.

NOTES: A fascinating species that exhibits both egg-laying and live-bearing reproductive methods depending on elevation.

REPRODUCTION: Reproductive mode varies geographically. In lowland coastal regions females lay eggs with varying calcium content in the shells; incubation period ranges from 5–30 days, depending on locality. In highlands above 1,000m females are viviparous, giving birth to fully developed young enclosed in a clear membrane, which the neonates break through shortly after birth.

Blotched Blue-tongue *Tiliqua nigrolutea*

PETER SOLTYS

STATUS: IUCN Least Concern; Urban Occurrence Rating ★★★★★

WHEN AND WHERE: Diurnal. Often basks in open areas in spring and autumn. In hotter months, activity tends to be limited to cooler mornings and late afternoons.

DESCRIPTION: SVL 300mm, TL 580mm. Rather long, thick tail and smooth scales. Ranges from brown to black, with large blotches that vary from whitish-yellow to pink or red and may be irregularly scattered or arranged in rows, forming bands along the tail. Northern populations tend to be darker and more reddish.

DISTRIBUTION ZONE: 4.

HABITAT: Woodlands, grasslands and rocky outcrops; also urban and rural areas with ground cover and shelter such as logs, leaf litter or garden mulch. Frequently seen in highland and cool-climate environments, particularly above 600m.

NOTES: Solitary and slow-moving. Relies on bluff for defence, opening mouth wide and extending blue tongue while hissing loudly. Diet consists of vegetation, invertebrates and carrion; plays an important role in controlling pests and cleaning up organic debris. Distinguished from Eastern Blue-tongue by blotched rather than banded pattern and choice of cooler, more elevated habitats.

REPRODUCTION: Up to 15 live young are born in late summer or early autumn.

Eastern Blue-tongue *Tiliqua scincoides*

ANDY MONCK

Status: IUCN Least Concern; Urban Occurrence Rating ★★★★☆

WHEN AND WHERE: Often basks in suburban gardens, bushland and parklands during spring and summer. Diurnal and often seen crossing paths, roads, or basking near structures in warm weather.

DESCRIPTION: SVL 320mm, TL 600mm. **Large**, robust skink with a broad head and distinctive bright **blue tongue**. Dorsal colour varies from yellow, brown or pale grey to black, with **six to nine dark-edged pale bands across back**. Broad dark stripe extends from eye to ear. Ventral surface can be white to grey or yellow.

DISTRIBUTION ZONES: 1, 2, 3, 4 and 5.

HABITAT: Highly adaptable. Common in urban areas and under backyard debris. Also found in open woodlands, dry forests and coastal heathlands. Seeks shelter under logs, rocks or dense shrubs, or within compost piles or leaf litter.

NOTES: Familiar and charismatic. Common in suburban gardens, where has a key role feeding on snails, slugs, insects, overripe fruit and carrion. Can puff up body, open mouth wide, and display blue tongue in dramatic defensive posture to deter predators. May be confused with Pink-tongued Skink or Blotched Blue-tongue.

REPRODUCTION: Gives birth to 10–15 live young in late summer or autumn.

South-eastern Slider *Lerista bougainvillii*

PETER SOLTYS

STATUS: IUCN Least Concern; Urban Occurrence Rating ★★★★★

WHEN AND WHERE: Most active in spring and summer. Secretive, often found by flipping leaf litter or logs.

DESCRIPTION: SVL 70mm, TL 150mm. Limbs highly reduced. Brown to grey body with **prominent black stripe along each side** and often narrower black stripes along the back, which may appear as dashed lines. Tail is speckled in adults and exhibit a reddish hue in juveniles. Scales smooth and glossy.

DISTRIBUTION ZONE: 4.

HABITAT: Found in sandy soils, leaf litter, grasslands, heath and open woodlands. Often shelters under rocks, logs or debris.

NOTES: Highly adapted for a fossorial (burrowing) lifestyle, using its reduced limbs and streamlined body to 'swim' through loose soil. Sometimes confused with legless lizards but can be distinguished by its small, vestigial limbs.

REPRODUCTION: Geographic variation in reproductive modes. Mainland populations lay eggs enclosed in a clear membrane containing almost fully developed young, which emerge shortly after deposition. Populations in Tasmania and on Kangaroo Island (South Australia) give birth to live young.

Jacky Dragon *Amphibolurus muricatus*

MARK SANDERS

STATUS: IUCN Least Concern; Urban Occurrence Rating ★★★☆☆

WHEN AND WHERE: Common throughout Sydney, particularly in dry sclerophyll forests. Most active in warmer months; often basks on logs, fences and rocks.

DESCRIPTION: SVL 120mm, TL 350mm. Robust, ground-dweller with long tail and spiny, laterally compressed body. **Pale to grey-brown with dark, jagged crossbands and often a pale vertebral stripe.** Three rows of sawtooth-like keeled scales line the back. Colour darkens when cold and lightens when warm. Long limbs aid fast movement. Male develops black throat patch when breeding.

DISTRIBUTION ZONES: 1, 3, 4 and 5.

HABITAT: Open woodlands, dry sclerophyll forests, heathlands and rocky ridges, with ground cover for shelter and sunny basking spots nearby. Often in areas disturbed by fire or clearing, where vegetation sparse and sun access high.

NOTES: Head-bobbing and push-up displays during territorial disputes. May flash yellow mouth lining as warning. Compare juvenile with Mountain Dragon.

REPRODUCTION: Oviparous. Up to eight eggs per clutch, with one or two clutches between October and February, laid in shallow nest in sandy or loamy soil, often in sunny clearing. Young emerge in early summer and are independent from birth.

Mountain Dragon *Rankinia diemensis*

MARK SANDERS

STATUS: IUCN Least Concern; Urban Occurrence Rating ★★★★★

WHEN AND WHERE: Active during the warmer months, commonly basking on rocks and logs in heathlands and open forests.

DESCRIPTION: SVL 84 mm, TL 200 mm. Blunt head with a large, visible eardrum and a blue mouth lining. Its body colour ranges from pale grey to reddish-brown, with spines along its back and at the base of its tail. **A row of pale, semi-circular markings run along its upper back, and a lighter stripe follows a skin fold down its sides and tail.** Its underside is cream.

DISTRIBUTION ZONE: 4.

HABITAT: Prefers cool-temperate woodlands, heathlands and rocky outcrops, often in areas with sparse ground cover.

NOTES: A cool-climate specialist, this is the only dragon living in regions with regular snowfall and the only one found in Tasmania, thriving in cool-temperate conditions.

May be confused with Jacky Dragon or Eastern Bearded Dragon; distinctive pink mouth-lining assists in differentiating it from the former.

REPRODUCTION: Up to nine eggs during the summer months and may produce multiple clutches in a season.

Angle-headed Dragon *Lophosaurus spinipes*

PETER SOLTYS

STATUS: IUCN Least Concern; Urban Occurrence Rating ★★★★★

WHEN AND WHERE: Most active from spring to early autumn. Diurnal but often remains motionless and well camouflaged, especially during warmer months when it basks in sunlit patches on tree trunks or rocks.

DESCRIPTION: SVL 110mm, TL 370mm. **Large, angular head with prominent spiny crest on back of head,** which continues along back. Colour varies from grey to grey-brown, often with a green tinge, and can change with temperature. A dark stripe usually runs from the eye to the exposed eardrum. Underside whitish.

DISTRIBUTION ZONE: 5.

HABITAT: Found primarily in rainforests, wet sclerophyll forests, and heavily vegetated gullies or rocky escarpments. Prefers vertical structures for basking and camouflage, often several metres off the ground.

NOTES: Agile and highly cryptic climber that freezes motionless when approached, blending into bark and foliage. While shy in the wild, it adapts well to forest-edge habitats, especially those with consistent humidity. Distinguished from juvenile Eastern Water Dragon or other arboreal agamids by its spiny crests.

REPRODUCTION: One or more clutches of 5–8 eggs in November and December.

Eastern Bearded Dragon *Pogona barbata*

ROB AMBROSE

STATUS: IUCN Least Concern; Urban Occurrence Rating ★★

WHEN AND WHERE: Increasingly difficult to find around Sydney due to inability to adapt to urban life. Still reasonably common on western fringe. Often basks on fence posts, rocks and tree trunks. Most active October to March.

DESCRIPTION: SVL to 260 mm, TL to 600 mm. Large grey to reddish-brown dragon with triangular head, spiny beard, keeled scales and dorsolateral stripes. Beard and chest can turn black during display.

DISTRIBUTION ZONES: 1.

HABITAT: Open woodland and dry sclerophyll forest with scattered logs, clearings, and trees for retreat. Often basks on warm bitumen after cool mornings, resulting in high number of traffic fatalities.

NOTES: Diurnal and alert. May gape when threatened, but usually runs for cover or climbs. Confusion species are Jacky Dragon or Eastern Water Dragon; expandable black beard and heavier build are distinctive.

REPRODUCTION: One to three clutches of 8–25 eggs laid in friable, sunny soil from October to January; hatch 60–80 days later depending on temperature. Hatchlings are independent immediately.

Eastern Water Dragon *Intellagama lesueurii*

MARK SANDERS

STATUS: IUCN Least Concern; Urban Occurrence Rating ★★★★★

WHEN AND WHERE: Most commonly seen in spring and summer. Often basks on rocks, walls and banks.

DESCRIPTION: SVL 245mm, TL 1,000mm. Australia's largest dragon lizard. Olive-brown to brown, with **dark stripe from eye to neck**, **dark bands on body** and **reddish tint on chest** that is more noticeable in breeding male. Key ID features include **strong limbs**, **long tail** and **prominent nuchal crest**.

DISTRIBUTION ZONES: 1, 2, 3, 4 and 5.

HABITAT: Common around freshwater creeks, rivers, ponds and wetlands. Frequent in suburban parks, botanic gardens and residential areas with water features and dense vegetation. Prefers places with both basking sites and quick access to water.

NOTES: Highly adapted to urban environments. Familiar sight in populated areas throughout eastern NSW. When threatened, typically dives into water and can remain submerged for up to 90 minutes. Exhibits social hierarchies – dominant males defend territories and maintain harems of females.

REPRODUCTION: Oviparous. Lays up to 18 eggs in sandy nest in November or December, with hatchlings emerging after about three months in late summer.

Heath Monitor *Varanus rosenbergi*

MARK SANDERS

STATUS: IUCN Least Concern; Urban Occurrence Rating ★★★★★

WHEN AND WHERE: Most active spring and summer, when seen basking or foraging.

DESCRIPTION: SVL 700mm, TL 1,600mm. Large, **robust, dark brown monitor** with **long claws** and **patterned with pale yellow or cream spots** forming irregular bands along body. Tail long and laterally compressed, featuring **distinctive alternating dark and light bands**. Head elongated with a pointed snout.

DISTRIBUTION ZONES: 1, 2 and 3.

HABITAT: Open heathlands, dry sclerophyll forests and rocky escarpments. Found throughout southern and south-eastern Australia, including uplands and coasts. Favours dense undergrowth, ground debris and basking spots such as logs or slabs.

NOTES: Often less bold than other monitors and quick to flee when approached. Tends to rely on retreat to hollow logs, burrows or dense scrub rather than bluff displays. Although superficially similar to the Lace Monitor, *V. rosenbergi* is darker, smaller, and lacks the prominent neck banding seen in *V. varius*.

REPRODUCTION: Oviparous. Lays up to 14 eggs in late summer, often in active termite mound. These provide stable heat and humidity, which support embryo development. Eggs incubate for an extended period, typically 6–9 months.

Lace Monitor *Varanus varius*

MARK SANDERS

STATUS: IUCN Least Concern; Urban Occurrence Rating ★★★★★

WHEN AND WHERE: Most active from spring to early autumn. Diurnal and often seen basking, foraging, or climbing trees.

DESCRIPTION: SVL 800mm, TL up to 2,100mm. Large with strong build, long limbs with sharp claws. Long, laterally compressed tail that is more than half total length. Ranges from black with cream spots to bold black and cream banding, with tail bands becoming broader towards tip. Dark stripe runs from snout through eye, bordered by pale yellow, and tongue is blue and forked.

Distribution zones: 1, 2, 3 and 4.

HABITAT: Open forests, woodlands and heath. Found near water, rock outcrops and urban edges. Often seen in picnic areas and along trails.

NOTES: Confident scavenger, often seen near campsites or bins. Climbs trees to raid nests or escape threats. May bluff with hissing or tail lashing when disturbed.

REPRODUCTION: Typically 10–12 eggs in active termite mounds, where stable temperature and humidity are ideal for incubation. Termites reseal chamber while eggs incubate, hatching in late summer or early autumn. Young remain in mound for weeks or months, and sometimes overwinter before emerging.

Blackish Blind Snake *Anilios nigrescens*

MARK SANDERS

VENOM RATING: Non-venomous
STATUS: IUCN Least Concern; Urban Occurrence Rating ★★★★☆
WHEN AND WHERE: Seen mostly in summer, often after heavy rain, when displaced from underground refuges. Frequent in gardens and compost heaps.
DESCRIPTION: TL 750mm. Small, worm-like snake with cylindrical body, smooth scales, blunt head that merges with neck, and point on tail tip. Tiny vestigial eyes appear as dark specks beneath skin. Mouth is set far back on rounded snout, making it almost imperceptible. Varies from dark brown to nearly black, often with purple sheen. May have small dark mark near vent. Male smaller than female.
DISTRIBUTION ZONES: 1, 2, 3, 4 and 5.
HABITAT: Moist, sandy environments, often in association with termite nests, decaying logs and leaf litter. Also in suburban gardens and urban greenspaces.
NOTES: Feeds almost exclusively on ant and termite larvae and pupae, using small but strong jaws to crush prey. If handled secretes musky fluid from cloacal glands as defence. Identification notoriously difficult, and beyond scope of this book.
REPRODUCTION: Mates late winter. Lays up to 15 eggs in mid- to late summer, often in communal nest sites beneath logs or rocks.

Woodland Blind Snake *Anilios proximus*

MARK SANDERS

VENOM RATING: Non-venomous

STATUS: IUCN Least Concern; Urban Occurrence Rating ★★★★★

WHEN AND WHERE: Most commonly seen during warm, wet periods in summer, particularly after rain when individuals are flushed from the soil.

DESCRIPTION: TL 750mm. Robust, cylindrical-bodied blind snake with blunt, slightly triangular snout when viewed from above. Head barely distinct from neck. Dorsal colouration varies from pinkish-brown to grey or dark brown, with contrasting pale yellowish-brown to cream underside. Small dark marking may be present near vent.

DISTRIBUTION ZONE: 5.

HABITAT: Varied, but especially sandy soils near ant and termite colonies. Frequently encountered in suburban gardens, beneath logs and in loose soil.

NOTES: Specialised diet of ant and termite larvae and pupae. Emits strong, musky defensive secretion when disturbed. Blind snake identification notoriously difficult, even for experts, and features required are beyond scope of this book.

REPRODUCTION: Mating in late winter. Females lay up to 15 eggs in communal nests beneath logs or rocks in mid- to late summer.

Brown-snouted Blind Snake *Anilios wiedii*

TOM FRISBY

VENOM RATING: **Non-venomous**

STATUS: IUCN Least Concern; Urban Occurrence Rating ★★★★★

WHEN AND WHERE: Mostly seen in summer, particularly on surface after rain.

DESCRIPTION: TL 300mm. Small, thin, worm-like snake with blunt, rounded snout. Dorsal surface bright pink to pinkish-brown, while ventral surface cream. Eyes reduced to dark spots beneath translucent scales. Dark streak usually visible on rostral scale at tip of snout.

DISTRIBUTION ZONE: 1.

HABITAT: Prefers loose, sandy soils and often associated with termite mounds and ant colonies. Found in dry sclerophyll forests, open woodlands and suburban gardens with mulch or compost.

NOTES: Feeds almost exclusively on ant and termite larvae and pupae. Like all blind snakes it produces a musky odour from cloacal glands when handled. Considered rare in the Greater Sydney region; it is more frequently encountered in suitable habitats in Queensland and northern New South Wales

REPRODUCTION: Mating takes place in late winter. Female lays clutch of up to 15 eggs in mid- to late summer, often in communal nest.

Brown Tree Snake *Boiga irregularis*

NILAN KUMARAGE

VENOM RATING: Venomous

STATUS: IUCN Least Concern; Urban Occurrence Rating ★★★★★

WHEN AND WHERE: Primarily nocturnal. Most active in warmer months, particularly after rain. Occasionally encountered indoors or on fences at night.

DESCRIPTION: TL 1,200mm average, 2,000mm maximum. Slender-bodied snake with a **clearly defined head and very large eyes with vertical pupils** – an adaptation to its nocturnal habits. Body reddish-brown, tan, or pale brown, with irregular darker crossbands along back. Underbelly cream to yellow, and tail long and prehensile to aid climbing.

Distribution zones: 1 and 2.

HABITAT: Varied, including woodlands, forests and urban areas. Often shelter in roof spaces, sheds and other structures in suburban settings.

NOTES: Possesses rear fangs and mild venom; may cause localised swelling if bitten but not considered dangerous to humans. Excellent climber, aided by prehensile tail. Feeds on birds, lizards, frogs, and small mammals.

REPRODUCTION: Breeds spring and summer. Females lay 3–12 eggs in moist, protected locations such as roof cavities, tree hollows or rock crevices.

Common Tree Snake *Dendrelaphis punctulatus*

JULES FARQUHAR

VENOM RATING: **Non-venomous**

STATUS: IUCN Least Concern; Urban Occurrence Rating ★★★★☆

WHEN AND WHERE: Diurnal, fast-moving, most active in warmer months. Often seen by bush tracks, in gardens, and sometimes indoors near water features.

DESCRIPTION: TL 1,800mm. Slender, fast-moving snake with large eyes and excellent vision. Can be bright green, gold and black, brown or blue-black. **In Sydney region, typically olive to dark green above with bright yellow to cream underside**. When threatened, expands body to reveal an iridescent pale blue between scales. Head narrow and distinct from neck.

DISTRIBUTION ZONES: 1, 2, 4 and 5.

HABITAT: Varied, including rainforests and woodlands; thrives in older suburban gardens where well-established greenery provides shelter and food.

NOTES: Active diurnal species with excellent eyesight. Often found in aggregations during cooler conditions.

REPRODUCTION: Lays clutch of up to 12 eggs. Communal nests common, including one record of more than 400 eggs in a single log, from multiple females over many years.

Corn Snake *Pantherophis guttatus*

ROB AMBROSE

VENOM RATING: **Non-venomous**

STATUS: **Introduced non-native species**; IUCN Least Concern (globally); NSW declared pest species; Urban Occurrence Rating ★★★★★

WHEN AND WHERE: Escaped or released pets may be found year-round.

DESCRIPTION: TL 1,200mm. Selective breeding has produced a range of colour variations, including red, grey, white and patterned forms. Underside usually has distinctive black-and-white checkerboard pattern. Eye round with reddish iris.

DISTRIBUTION ZONE: 1.

HABITAT: Highly adaptable and capable of surviving in bushland, farmlands and urban areas. Prefers areas with abundant small mammal prey.

NOTES: Often mistaken for native snake species. Native to south-eastern USA, but released or escaped individuals found in NSW, primarily in Sydney's outer suburbs. No evidence yet of established population, but ongoing monitoring required. Like all exotic reptiles it is illegal to keep in NSW. Escaped or released individuals pose a threat by potentially competing with native species.

REPRODUCTION: Lays clutch of 10–30 eggs in summer, hatching after about 60 days. In warmer climates, females may produce two clutches per year.

Diamond Python *Morelia spilota*

CHRIS WILLIAMS

VENOM RATING: **Non-venomous**, although large pythons can still inflict serious bites.

STATUS: IUCN Least Concern; Urban Occurrence Rating ★★★★★

WHEN AND WHERE: Most active in warmer months from September and February. Often seen crossing roads, basking on verandas, or curled up in sheds and gardens. Mating activity peaks in spring, with feeding becoming focus by late summer.

DESCRIPTION: TL up to 2,500mm. Variable, with **dark olive to black base and yellow or cream spots on most dorsal scales**. Spots cluster into rosettes, which are larger but fewer in south and more vibrant north of Gosford. Intergrades with Coastal Carpet Python (subspecies *mcdowelli*) on NSW Mid North Coast.

DISTRIBUTION ZONES: 1, 2, 3, 4 and 5.

HABITAT: Varied; rainforest, dry sclerophyll forest, coastal heathland, escarpments and subalpine areas. One of few large reptiles to persist in leafy suburban areas, feeding on possums. Common in national parks and bushland edges.

NOTES: Docile. Not dangerous to humans.

REPRODUCTION: Male travels far in search of mate, with much competition. Female coils body around 15-30 eggs to incubate them; they hatch after two months.

Common Death Adder *Acanthophis antarcticus*

SEAN CADE

VENOM RATING: Highly Venomous

STATUS: IUCN Least Concern; Urban Occurrence Rating ★★★★★

WHEN AND WHERE: Most common in Central Coast, Hawkesbury and Sutherland Shire. Often seen crossing roads on warm evenings, particularly after rainfall. Remains motionless during day, camouflaged among leaf litter.

DESCRIPTION: TL 700mm average, 1,200mm maximum. Thick-bodied, short-tailed viper-like snake with triangular head distinctly wider than neck. Body heavily banded; grey morph and red morph found in Sydney region, both with darker crossbands. Tail tip is usually paler, with small, curved spur.

DISTRIBUTION ZONES: 1, 4 and 5.

HABITAT: Sandy soils in coastal heathlands, dense scrub and dry sclerophyll forests.

NOTES: Tail tip acts as **caudal lure**, mimicking small worm to attract prey. Unlike most elapids it is an ambush predator, using camouflage and staying motionless in leaf litter. Despite potent neurotoxic venom, bites are rare due to reclusive nature.

REPRODUCTION: Gives birth to up to 30 live young in late summer. Neonates are fully independent at birth.

Highlands Copperhead *Austrelaps ramsayii*

TOM FRISBY

VENOM RATING: Highly Venomous

STATUS: IUCN Least Concern; Urban Occurrence Rating ★★★★★

WHEN AND WHERE: Blue Mountains, particularly in cooler, wetter habitats. Most active on mild days in late spring and summer.

DESCRIPTION: TL 1,100mm. Moderately heavy body with broad, slightly distinct head. **Upper labial scales boldly patterned with alternating black and white bars.** Dorsal varies from pale grey to dark charcoal, often with coppery wash across crown and nape. Ventral surface pale grey to creamy yellow. Fine, dark vertebral line often visible, particularly in juvenile. Contrasting lip markings include pale, triangular patches towards front of mouth, grading into darker posterior scales.

DISTRIBUTION ZONES: 3 and 4.

HABITAT: Swamps, sedgelands, wet sclerophyll forests and marshy clearings. Common near water bodies in Blue Mountains and Southern Tablelands.

NOTES: One of the few Australian snakes that can remain active in cold weather. Feeds mainly on frogs but also preys on lizards and small mammals. Juvenile may be mistaken for White-lipped Snake or Eastern Small-eyed Snake.

REPRODUCTION: Gives birth to up to 25 young between January and March.

Dwarf Crowned Snake *Cacophis krefftii*

MARK SANDERS

VENOM RATING: Venomous

STATUS: IUCN Least Concern; Urban Occurrence Rating ★★★★★

WHEN AND WHERE: Blue Mountains, Central Coast ranges and Watagans. Primarily nocturnal and most active on warm, humid nights, particularly following rain. Most frequently encountered from spring through to early autumn.

DESCRIPTION: TL 345mm. Small, slender snake with smooth, glossy scales. Dark steel-grey to black above. **Narrow yellow collar extends across back of neck and onto sides of head.** Belly white, with black stripe along underside of tail. Head rounded and indistinct from neck. Eyes small. Female slightly larger than male.

DISTRIBUTION ZONE: 5.

HABITAT: Coastal and upland wet forests, including rainforest, moist sclerophyll forest and vine thickets. Prefers damp microhabitats such as beneath leaf litter, rotting logs or rocks, or among debris in shaded, moist areas.

NOTES: Can be found in large breeding congregations with dozens of individuals. Primarily feeds on skinks and small frogs.

REPRODUCTION: Lays up to five relatively large eggs in January, that hatch in March.

Golden-crowned Snake *Cacophis squamulosus*

BOTH IMAGES: CHRIS WILLIAMS

VENOM RATING: Venomous

STATUS: IUCN Least Concern; Urban Occurrence Rating ★★★★★

WHEN AND WHERE: Most active on warm, humid nights from spring through autumn. Commonly seen in Sydney's leafy suburbs, especially following rain.

DESCRIPTION: TL 500mm average, 750mm maximum. Small to medium-sized with slender build and smooth, glossy scales. Dorsal dark brown to grey. **Yellowish or light tan band runs from above each eye and across snout, meeting a broader stripe across the nape** but not forming a complete collar. Head distinctly angular and broader than neck. Ventral surface strikingly reddish, particularly near tail.

DISTRIBUTION ZONES: 1, 2, 3, 4 and 5.

HABITAT: Has adapted well to urban environments. Found in sclerophyll forests, riparian zones, wet temperate forests and open woodlands.

NOTES: Can be mistaken for the Dwarf Crowned Snake or Marsh Snake due to similar size and markings. Preys on small reptiles, skink eggs and frogs. Frequently observed crossing paths or driveways at night.

REPRODUCTION: Female lays up to 15 eggs in January, which hatch in March.

Yellow-faced Whip Snake *Demansia psammophis*

MAIN IMAGE: JULES FARQUHAR; INSET: TOM FRISBY

VENOM RATING: Venomous
STATUS: IUCN Least Concern; Urban Occurrence Rating ★★★☆☆
WHEN AND WHERE: Active during warmer months. A diurnal species, frequently observed moving swiftly across open ground.
DESCRIPTION: TL 1,000mm. Pale grey, blue-grey or olive, often with two reddish stripes running from behind neck to front third of body. **Large brown margin around eye, with bold pale edges in front and behind that sweep back towards mouth, forming comma-shape.** Thin dark line runs across snout between nostrils.
DISTRIBUTION ZONES: 1, 4 and 5.
HABITAT: Variety of dry habitats including coastal heath, dry sclerophyll forest, inland woodland and open scrubland; also rocky hillsides and near grassy clearings. Occasionally in suburban gardens next to areas of bush.
NOTES: A fast-moving and highly alert diurnal hunter. Possesses excellent vision. May be confused with Eastern Brown Snake.
REPRODUCTION: Mates in late winter and spring. Lay clutches of up to 10 eggs in early summer. Communal nest sites are known and one, used over several seasons, held over 500 eggs. Young hatch in late February and March.

White-lipped Snake *Drysdalia coronoides*

MAIN IMAGE: MARK SANDERS; INSET: JULES FARQUHAR

VENOM RATING: Venomous

STATUS: IUCN Least Concern; Urban Occurrence Rating ★★★★★

WHEN AND WHERE: Active during warmer months, but prefers cooler conditions. Often found sunning itself in the early morning, late afternoon, or on cooler days.

DESCRIPTION: TL 450mm. Small snake with deep, narrow head slightly distinct from neck. **Thin white stripe runs along upper lip from snout to side of neck.** Body colour varies from light grey to nearly black, with a yellow, cream or pink underside.

DISTRIBUTION ZONE: 3.

HABITAT: Occurs at higher altitudes in Greater Sydney region, including Blue Mountains and Illawarra Plateau.

NOTES: Australia's most cold-tolerant snake. Feeds primarily on small skinks. May be confused with Marsh Snake, Mustard-bellied Snake or juvenile Highlands Copperhead.

REPRODUCTION: Live-bearing, with female giving birth to up to 10 young between late summer and mid-autumn.

Mustard-bellied Snake *Drysdalia rhodogaster*

BRIAN LA RANCE

VENOM RATING: Venomous
STATUS: IUCN Least Concern; Urban Occurrence Rating ★★★★★
WHEN AND WHERE: Blue Mountains, Central Coast ranges; cryptic and uncommon.
DESCRIPTION: TL 400mm.Small, slender snake with brown to olive-grey body, darker on top of head. **Distinctive orange to yellow band runs across neck and narrow dark line extends from nostril to eye**, but lacks a white stripe along upper lip. Scales are smooth, and body shape is moderately robust.
DISTRIBUTION ZONE: 4.
HABITAT: Tussock grass-dominated woodland and open forest. Prefers areas with dense ground cover, where it can remain hidden beneath vegetation and leaf litter.
NOTES: Highly secretive and rarely seen, even in known range. Preys mostly on small lizards using ambush tactics. When disturbed, may flatten body slightly as defensive display. Compare with Marsh Snake and White-lipped Snake. Genus *Drysdalia* named by herpetologist Eric Worrell in honour of his artist friend Russell Drysdale.
REPRODUCTION: Live-bearing species, giving birth to an average of five young per litter. Birthing occurs over the summer months.

Red-naped Snake *Furina diadema*

MARK SANDERS

VENOM RATING: Venomous

STATUS: IUCN Least Concern; Urban Occurrence Rating ★★★☆☆

WHEN AND WHERE: Nocturnal. Most often seen on bushland roads or footpaths on warm, humid nights, especially during late summer and early autumn.

DESCRIPTION: TL 400mm. Small, glossy, smooth-scaled, slender elapid. Dorsal reddish-brown to dark chocolate brown or orange-brown, with black-edged scales creating subtle reticulated pattern. Most distinctive feature is **black 'hood' or nape marking edged with reddish or orange-red crescent**. Belly white to pinkish.

DISTRIBUTION ZONE: 4.

HABITAT: Variety of environments including dry woodlands, grasslands, mallee scrub and inland arid areas. Prefers microhabitats with ample ground cover such as rocks, bark and leaf litter, and also found in suburban yards near bush edges.

NOTES: Secretive and generally placid, this snake rarely bites when handled. Although mildly venomous, it poses minimal risk to humans. Feeds primarily on small skinks and their eggs. May be confused with juvenile Eastern Brown Snake, but can be distinguished by its black-and-red neck marking and smaller size.

REPRODUCTION: Female typically lays clutch of 3–4 eggs during warmer months.

Marsh Snake *Hemiaspis signata*

MAIN IMAGE: LUCAS WILLIAMS; INSET: CHRIS WILLIAMS

VENOM RATING: **Venomous.** Mildly venomous – a bite may cause localised swelling or discomfort, but not considered dangerous to humans.

STATUS: IUCN Least Concern; Urban Occurrence Rating ★★★★★

WHEN AND WHERE: Primarily active in warmer months, especially spring and summer. Often seen following rainfall and during periods of high humidity.

DESCRIPTION: TL 700mm. Dorsal colour ranges from grey to dark brown or olive, sometimes with reddish tinge. Ventral surface dark, often black or dark grey. Head features **two distinct pale stripes on each side: one runs from snout through eye to side of neck, and the other curves along upper lip to mouth corner**. These markings are key distinguishing features.

DISTRIBUTION ZONES: 1, 2, 3, 4 and 5.

HABITAT: Moist environments such as swamps, marshes, creek edges, wet sclerophyll forests and floodplains. Occasionally found in urban parklands and gardens, especially near water sources.

NOTES: May be mistaken for Mustard-bellied Snake, although head markings help with identification. Feeds on frogs, tadpoles and small reptiles.

REPRODUCTION: Has one litter of up to 20 offspring per year in late summer.

Broad-headed Snake *Hoplocephalus bungaroides*

JULES FARQUHAR

VENOM RATING: Highly Venomous

STATUS: IUCN Endangered; Urban Occurrence Rating ★★★★★

WHEN AND WHERE: Most active from late spring to summer. Primarily nocturnal, sheltering in narrow sandstone rock crevices during day and hunting at night.

DESCRIPTION: TL 900mm. **Black above with many narrow, irregular, bright yellow bands** that are bold towards front and become fainter along body and tail. Head broad and flat with large eyes, aiding identification. Patterning can resemble that of harmless Diamond Python, which occurs in overlapping habitat.

DISTRIBUTION ZONES: 3 and 4.

HABITAT: Restricted to sandstone outcrops, rock ledges and dry sclerophyll forests, particularly in Sydney Basin and Blue Mountains. Daytime refuge is taken in exfoliating sandstone slabs or tree hollows.

NOTES: Highly habitat-specific and severely impacted by rock removal. Very low reproductive rate makes it vulnerable to habitat degradation and fire.

REPRODUCTION: Mates from autumn to spring, with 12 young born between January and April every two to three years.

Pale-headed Snake *Hoplocephalus bitorquatus*

TIM FAULKNER

VENOM RATING: Highly Venomous

STATUS: IUCN Least Concern; Urban Occurrence Rating ★★★★★

WHEN AND WHERE: Most active during warmer months, particularly on humid nights. Rarely seen during day due to secretive and arboreal habits.

DESCRIPTION: TL 800mm. Slender with **characteristic pale grey to creamy white head and neck area.** Wide pale collar stretches across back of neck, bordered behind by a solid or broken black bar, and in front by angular dark blotches extending towards snout. Rest of body ranges from grey to dark brown or black, sometimes with faint banding. Eyes relatively large and forward-facing.

DISTRIBUTION ZONE: 5.

HABITAT: Found in eucalypt woodland, dry sclerophyll forest and rainforest margins. Prefers areas with access to trees and logs, often near watercourses.

NOTES: Arboreal and nocturnal, frequently found in tree hollows, under bark, or in dense shrubs. Feeds primarily on tree frogs and small lizards, and occasionally on small mammals. Considered rare in Greater Sydney region, with southern limit of distribution reaching to around Gosford.

REPRODUCTION: Females give birth to litters of up to 10 live young.

Stephens' Banded Snake *Hoplocephalus stephensii*

MARK SANDERS

VENOM RATING: Highly Venomous

STATUS: IUCN Least Concern; Urban Occurrence Rating ★★★★★

WHEN AND WHERE: Nocturnal. Active September to May. Rarely seen due to secretive nature and preference for dense forest.

DESCRIPTION: TL 1,200mm. **Dark grey with many narrow brown or orange bands** that fade and become less visible towards back. Sometimes bands connect to form figure-of-eight pattern, others lack any bands at all. Sides of head often blotched or striped with black and white, but sometimes head lacks any markings.

DISTRIBUTION ZONE: 5.

HABITAT: Rainforest, wet sclerophyll forest and vine scrub. Shelters in tree hollows or under loose bark or dense understorey. Arboreal; often 20 metres up in canopy.

NOTES: Nervous and defensive temperament when threatened. These adept climbers use their slender bodies and specialised ventral scales with lateral notches to grip onto branches. Actively hunts or ambushes small mammals, lizards and frogs. Range extends south to around Gosford; considered rare in the region.

REPRODUCTION: Litter of 3–8 young born in February or March every two or three years; this low reproductive output is characteristic of the genus.

Eastern Small-eyed Snake *Cryptophis nigrescens*

SHANE BLACK

VENOM RATING: **Highly Venomous.** Venom can cause muscle damage, pain, and, in severe cases, renal failure. At least one human fatality attributed to its bite. Immediate medical attention essential if bitten.

STATUS: IUCN Least Concern; Urban Occurrence Rating ★★★☆☆

WHEN AND WHERE: Nocturnal. Frequently found on roads at night, especially in warmer months. Common but secretive, so often goes unnoticed.

DESCRIPTION: TL 500mm average, 1,000mm maximum. Uniformly glossy black snake with no visible pattern. Underside cream to pale pink, with colour restricted to belly scales, not extending onto lower sides of body.

DISTRIBUTION ZONES: 2, 3, 4 and 5.

HABITAT: Diverse range of environments, including rainforest, wet and dry sclerophyll forests, woodlands, heathlands and rocky outcrops. During day seeks shelter under rocks or logs, or among leaf litter or other ground debris.

NOTES: Preys on small skinks. Confusable with juvenile Red-bellied Black Snake.

REPRODUCTION: Viviparous, giving birth to live young. Females typically produce litters of 2–4 offspring during late summer to early autumn.

Red-bellied Black Snake *Pseudechis porphyriacus*

GARY STEPHENSON

VENOM RATING: Highly Venomous
STATUS: IUCN Least Concern; Urban Occurrence Rating ★★★★☆
WHEN AND WHERE: Most active during day, particularly in spring and early summer. Frequently seen basking near water courses.
DESCRIPTION: TL 2,000mm. Glossy black upper body with distinctive red to pinkish lower flank and belly, which fades to lighter cream or orange near tail.
DISTRIBUTION ZONES: 1, 2, 3, 4 and 5.
HABITAT: Has adapted well to urban environments. Prefers wetlands, swamps, riverbanks and woodlands, but also found in suburban areas near water.
NOTES: Despite fearsome reputation, generally shy and prefers to escape rather than attack. One of the few snakes that will prey on other venomous snakes, including Eastern Brown Snake. No human fatalities have been recorded. Juvenile may be confused with Eastern Small-eyed Snake and Golden crowned Snake.
REPRODUCTION: Mates in spring; male combat often observed. Pregnant females often gather in same shelter site. Up to 20 young born around late summer.

Eastern Brown Snake *Pseudonaja textilis*

MAIN IMAGE: CHRIS WILLIAMS; INSET: ROB HYNSON

VENOM RATING: Highly Venomous

STATUS: IUCN Least Concern; Urban Occurrence Rating ★★★★☆

WHEN AND WHERE: Active from spring to autumn, primarily during the day. Most encounters with humans occur in the warmer months.

DESCRIPTION: TL 1,500mm average, 2,500mm maximum. Ranges from light tan to dark brown, sometimes with faint banding. Belly pale cream, often speckled with orange or grey. Juvenile has more distinct markings, often with black head, dark band across nape, and, in Sydney region, strong banding along body.

DISTRIBUTION ZONES: 1, 3 and 4.

HABITAT: Open forest, grassland and farmland. Frequent in urban areas.

NOTES: Highly adaptable and known for its speed and defensive aggression when threatened; raises forebody, flattens neck, and may strike repeatedly. Responsible for majority of snakebite fatalities in Australia. Despite reputation, avoids human interaction whenever possible.

REPRODUCTION: Males fighting for access to females. Clutch of 10–35 eggs (average about 16) laid in late spring or early summer in sheltered location such as burrow, hollow log or under debris; hatching after about two or three months.

Tiger Snake *Notechis scutatus*

PETER SOLTYS

VENOM RATING: Highly Venomous

STATUS: IUCN Least Concern; Urban Occurrence Rating ★★★★★

WHEN AND WHERE: Mostly diurnal but may also be active on warm summer nights. Now uncommon in metropolitan Sydney but remains locally common in Blue Mountains and cooler, wetter areas. Sightings peak in spring and summer when they bask and search for prey or mates.

DESCRIPTION: TL 1,200mm. The head is broad and noticeably distinct from the neck. Colour and pattern can be highly variable but, in the Sydney region, they are typically marked with subdued bands of tan, brown and grey. Their faces often feature darker bands, and a yellow tint is often visible along their sides.

DISTRIBUTION ZONES: 3, 4 and 5.

HABITAT: Favours wetter habitats such as swamps, streams, riverbanks and wet sclerophyll forests, where frogs and small mammals are abundant.

NOTES: Historically responsible for many snakebite fatalities, but incidents have declined in populated areas. May be confused with Highlands Copperhead.

REPRODUCTION: Usually, 15–30 live young are born in late summer, although larger litter sizes have been recorded.

Common Bandy Bandy *Vermicella annulata*

MARK SANDERS

VENOM RATING: Venomous

STATUS: IUCN Least Concern; Urban Occurrence Rating ★★★★★

WHEN AND WHERE: Primarily nocturnal. Most frequently seen on warm, humid summer nights, particularly after rain. Often seen crossing roads or under surface debris in bushland areas. Sightings peak from late spring through to early autumn.

DESCRIPTION: TL 500–600mm average, 800mm maximum. This visually distinctive species is characterised by smooth, glossy scales arranged in striking black and white bands that completely encircle the body. It has a short, blunt tail and a head that is only subtly distinct from the neck. In a defensive display, it raises sections of its body into high, looping coils to confuse or deter predators.

DISTRIBUTION ZONES: 1, 2, 3, 4 and 5.

HABITAT: Open woodlands, heaths and sandy soils, often under rocks and logs.

NOTES: Specialist predator that feeds almost exclusively on blind snakes (family *Anilios*), making it one of the few known ophiophagous (snake-eating) elapids in Australia. While venomous, it poses little risk to humans due to its small fangs and reclusive nature.

REPRODUCTION: Clutch sizes average around seven eggs but can range up to 13.

Yellow-bellied Sea Snake *Hydrophis platurus*

GARY DUNNETT

VENOM RATING: Highly Venomous

STATUS: IUCN Least Concern; Urban Occurrence Rating N/A

WHEN AND WHERE: Truly pelagic species found throughout tropical and subtropical oceans worldwide. Individuals occasionally recorded in NSW when warm tropical currents push south during summer and autumn. Strandings occur along much of east coast, particularly after storms or sustained northerly flow.

DESCRIPTION: TL to 1,000 mm. Body slender and laterally compressed, with distinct paddle-shaped tail adapted for swimming. Dorsal surface dark brown to jet black; ventral surface bright yellow extending onto tail, forming a sharp contrast. Scales small, juxtaposed and faintly keeled, giving body a smooth, satiny texture.

DISTRIBUTION ZONES: 1, 2 and 5 (vagrant).

HABITAT: Open ocean; occasionally drifts into sheltered coastal waters via East Australian Current. Unable to move effectively on land.

NOTES: Feeds mainly on small surface-dwelling fish. Breathes air but capable of remaining submerged for more than two hours. Individuals stranded in Sydney region often weakened by cold water and rarely survive, although some have been successfully rehabilitated and released.

REPRODUCTION: Ovoviviparous. Gives birth at sea to 2–6 fully formed young.

About the Authors

Chris Williams has been a member of the Australian Herpetological Society since 1985 and has served as President for the past decade. He worked in the reptile departments of both Taronga Zoo and the Australian Reptile Park before stepping away from the field – although he would later go on to own Snake Ranch, Australia's largest breeding facility for reptiles, catering to hobbyists specialising in python morphs.

In 2023, Chris founded Urban Reptile Removal, a company specialising in the removal of unwanted snakes and other reptiles across the Sydney region. He now works full-time as a snake catcher, spending his days – and many nights – relocating reptiles from homes and businesses throughout the city.

Chris's primary interest lies in urban reptiles, and how the shifting landscape of Greater Sydney has created both winners and losers among the region's reptile species and how different species adapt – or fail to adapt – to a rapidly evolving urban environment. This is Chris's sixth book.

Tim Faulkner is a leading Australian conservationist, zookeeper and wildlife advocate dedicated to protecting Australia's unique fauna. As the Managing Director of Aussie Ark, he has spearheaded critical conservation projects focused on endangered species recovery, habitat restoration and breeding programs for threatened wildlife.

With decades of hands-on experience in wildlife management, Tim has been instrumental in saving species like the Tasmanian Devil and helping to secure the future of lesser-known but equally vital reptiles. His deep passion for reptiles, coupled with a commitment to ethical herping and conservation, has made him a trusted voice in Australian herpetology.

Beyond his conservation work, Tim is a well-known wildlife educator and media personality, using his platform to inspire the next generation of nature enthusiasts. His dedication to reptile conservation shines through in this book, offering readers a fascinating and responsible insight into Sydney's reptile diversity. Tim is co-owner and director of the award-winning Australian Reptile Park he calls home.

References

Animalia.bio. (n.d.). *Burton's legless lizard.* https://www.animalia.bio/burtons-legless-lizard

Animalia.bio. (n.d.). *Common scaly-foot.* https://www.animalia.bio/pygopus-lepidopodus

Animalia.bio. (n.d.). *Underwoodisaurus milii.* https://www.animalia.bio/underwoodisaurus-milii

Atlas of Living Australia. (n.d.). *Species profiles.* https://bie.ala.org.au

Australian Museum. (n.d.). *Reptiles.* https://australian.museum/learn/animals/reptiles

Australian Museum. (n.d.). *Snakes, lizards and other reptiles.* https://australian.museum/learn/animals/reptiles/snakes-lizards-and-other-reptiles

Aussie Animals. (n.d.). *Australian Reptiles: Guide to Australia's Cold-Blooded Creatures.* https://aussieanimals.com/australian-reptiles

Australian Reptile Online Database (AROD). (n.d.). *Home.* https://arod.com.au

Central Queensland Coast Landcare Network. (n.d.). *Tree-base litter skink.* https://cqclandcarenetwork.org.au/wildlife/tree-base-litter-skink

Cogger, H.G. (1986). *Reptiles and Amphibians of Australia* (4th Ed.). Reed Books.

Cogger, H.G. (2014). *Reptiles and Amphibians of Australia* (7th Ed.). CSIRO Publishing.

Department of Climate Change, Energy, the Environment and Water (DCCEEW). (n.d.). *NSW BioNet Atlas.* https://www.environment.nsw.gov.au

Ehmann, H. (1992). *Encyclopedia of Australian Animals: Reptiles.* Angus & Robertson.

Gow, G.F. (1989). *Graeme Gow's Complete Guide to Australian Snakes.* Angus & Robertson.

Greer, A.E. (1997). *The Biology and Evolution of Australian Lizards.* Surrey Beatty & Sons.

IUCN Red List of Threatened Species. (2024). *Species assessments.* https://www.iucnredlist.org

Kiddle Encyclopedia. (n.d.). *Burton's legless lizard.* https://kids.kiddle.co/Burton%27s_legless_lizard

King, D., and Green, B. (1999). *Goanna: The Biology of Varanid Lizards.* Kreiger Publishing.

Museums Victoria. (n.d.). *Species records and fact sheets.* https://collections.museumsvictoria.com.au

OzAnimals. (n.d.). *Weasel Skink.* https://www.ozanimals.com/Reptile/Weasel-Skink/Saproscincus/mustelinus.html

Shea, G. (1998). *The Distribution and Status of the Broad-headed Snake, Hoplocephalus bungaroides.* Australian Nature Conservation Agency.

Shea, G. (2004). *The Reptiles of the Northern Rivers*. Northern Rivers Catchment Management Authority.

Shea, G., and Sadlier, R. (1999). *A Field Guide to the Reptiles of the Sydney Region*. Surrey Beatty & Sons.

Shine, R. (1973). Habitat requirements and conservation of the Broad-headed Snake, *Hoplocephalus bungaroides*. *Biological Conservation* 5(2): 121–132.

Shine, R. (1974). Reproduction, growth and sexual dimorphism in Australian elapid snakes. *Herpetologica* 30(2): 233–245.

Shine, R. (1976). Sexual size dimorphism and male combat in snakes. *Oecologia* 27(3): 289–291.

Shine, R. (1977). Habitat requirements of the Pig-nosed Turtle, *Carettochelys insculpta*. *Herpetologica* 33(3): 302–307.

Shine, R. (1980). Ecology of the Australian Death Adder *Acanthophis antarcticus*. *Journal of Herpetology* 14(2): 129–137.

Shine, R. (1998). *Australian Snakes: A Natural History*. Reed Hew Holland.

Shine, R. (1998). Reproductive biology and diet of the Bandy Bandy Snake (*Vermicella annulata*). *Journal of Herpetology* 18(3): 246–252.

Shine, R., and Covacevich, J. (1983). Ecological characteristics of *Enhydris polylepis* (Serpentes: Homalopsinae), a tropical Australian freshwater snake. *Journal of Herpetology* 17(2): 150–154.

Shine, R., Harlow, P.S., and Keogh, J.S. (1996). Commercial harvesting of giant lizards: The biology of water monitors (*Varanus salvator*) in southern Sumatra. *Biological Conservation* 77(2–3): 125–134.

Storr, G.M., Smith, L.A., and Johnstone, R.E. (1981). *Snakes of Western Australia*. Western Australian Museum.

Swan, G., Shea, G., and Sadlier, R. (2022). *A Field Guide to Reptiles of New South Wales* (4th Ed.). Reed New Holland.

The Animal Facts. (n.d.). *Burton's legless lizard*. https://www.theanimalfacts.com/reptiles/burtons-legless-lizard

Tilligerry Habitat. (n.d.). *Weasel skink*. https://www.tilligerryhabitat.au/weasel-skink

Webb, J.K., and Shine, R. (1998). Ecological characteristics of a threatened snake species, *Hoplocephalus bungaroides* (Elapidae), and the sympatric non-threatened *Hoplocephalus stephensii*. *Wildlife Research* 25(6): 585–598.

Wikipedia contributors. (n.d.). *Various species entries. Wikipedia*. https://en.wikipedia.org

Wilson, S.K., and Swan, G. (2025). *A Complete Guide to Reptiles of Australia* (7th Ed.). Reed New Holland.

Wildlife Tourism Australia. (n.d.). *Reptiles of Australia*. https://www.wildlifetourism.org.au/wildlife/reptiles-of-australia

Index